KINGDOM

GB-004

Designed by Add Graphics
P.O. Box 15
Waterlooville PO7 6BQ
England

Published by Kingdom Books
P.O. Box 15
Waterlooville PO7 6BQ
England

Persian Cats

Marianne Mays

Persian Cats

This book is dedicated to Blondie, who started it all, and to her daughter, Bella, who sadly died young.

Together their names form my breeding prefix, BlondBella.

Acknowledgements

Many thanks to the GCCF for letting me use their standards, to Shaun Flannery for putting up with odd photograph requests, and to Val Robinson for letting us use her beautiful cats as photographic models. One of Val's kittens, the little Blue-point male in the "growing kitten" sequence, actually won Best In Show (kitten male) at his first-ever show. Thank you also to everybody else who helped me in one way or another with this book.

contents

foreword

I used to think that cats were boring. They were creatures that slept, ate, and occasionally batted a piece of screwed up paper around. Their only real interest in life was food, and they were not very affectionate. These views were mainly based on my own cat, a non-pedigree Tabby called Felix. Today, more than 17 years later, Felix is still a cat who is mainly interested in food and rest, with affection for a select few - when he feels like it! But I have learnt that not all cats are like Felix.

I first began to suspect that Felix was not a representative feline when I started working as a veterinary nurse in my home country of Sweden. The vet for whom I worked was a cat lover, Persians being her favourite breed. Consequently many Persian breeders visited her surgery. Through her I met Persians of all shapes, colours and ages, and I gradually realised that these cats were different. Here was an affectionate, playful breed of cat, whose enjoyment of life went far beyond food and sleep. Though I was to learn that this was true of many other breeds, it was the Persian which particularly stuck in my mind. Not only were they playful, friendly and affectionate, but they were also extremely beautiful, with their long fluffy coats in such a variety of colours. It was then that I decided that one day I would have a Persian of my own.

At the time, however, I was still 16 years old and living at home with my mother, who would not hear of another cat in the house. To be fair, I very much doubt that Felix would have accepted such an intruder. So it was to be six long years before I finally got my dream cat: a Persian.

I was an avid collector of animal picture postcards, always on the lookout for new additions to my collection. One day, out shopping in Sweden, I found a card showing the most beautiful cat I had ever seen. It was a Persian, pale cream in colour, with face mask, ears, legs and tail in darker cream, and sapphire blue eyes. I bought the card, deciding on the spot that this was to be what my own first Persian cat would look like, but it was some months before I succeeded in identifying it as a Cream Colourpoint.

Years later, I was able to realise my dream. I had just moved to England to get married, and my husband and I were living in a small studio flat in London. Forced to leave my dog behind in Sweden, I desperately wanted to replace my companion and pet. (He later joined me in England - but that is a different story.) However, pets were not allowed in the block of flats in which we lived. I reckoned that although it may be impossible to keep a dog secret, a cat was less likely to be discovered. Our landlord was working abroad, so he was unlikely to drop in. My husband, although doubtful at first, went along with my plans. His main concern was that someone might spot a cat sitting at one of our windows. As the flat was on the third floor, I felt this was improbable, but as a precaution I placed a large assortment of stuffed toy animals in the main window, hoping that passers by would not be able to tell one furry face from another! It must have worked, because nobody ever remarked upon our cat.

All that remained was to find a suitable kitten. I knew exactly what I wanted: a Cream Colourpoint Persian cat. We had almost given up hope of finding one when one day I spotted an advertisement for Cream Colourpoint kittens in Cats magazine. I bought one of the kittens, and so Blondie became my very first Persian. The six-year wait proved worthwhile, as Blondie was and still is one of the nicest pets I have ever owned - and I have had hundreds! Blondie was not boring in any way. As playful as anything, she soon became my constant companion. Her early tricks included climbing up my trouser leg whilst I was cooking dinner, just to check on what I was doing, and waking my husband in the morning by prodding his face with a paw if she felt we had overslept. Today she is a great-grandmother who adores nothing more than looking after kittens, even though they are not her own. Blondie is just a pet, not a show cat, but she is very special, and the sole reason why our house is now home to 15 cats, mainly Persians. Never again will I think cats are boring!

foreword

This book is for people like me, who want a Persian cat as a companion and pet. Although it also explains the basics of showing and breeding, it is primarily intended for the average pet owner. I do hope that you are reading this book before purchasing a Persian cat as a pet, for Persians can be quite demanding, especially when it comes to caring for their coats. If you are not prepared to spend a good deal of time grooming, then a Persian is not the pet for you; nor are they ideal for very house-proud people, intolerant of cat hairs. It is very important to realise this before a Persian arrives in your home, or neither you nor your cat will be happy.

Throughout this book, topics such as different colour varieties of the Persian cat and show procedures are described in the way set down by the Governing Council of the Cat Fancy (GCCF). The GCCF is the largest governing body of the cat fancy in Britain and the oldest in the world, and it is for this reason that I have referred to its guidelines. Although there are other governing bodies in Britain and America, with many differing rules and traditions, this book is written from the GCCF point of view. This should be borne in mind throughout, especially with regard to the chapter on showing.

Marianne Mays

Persian Cats

history & development 1

Longhaired cats are probably the result of a genetic mutation. They have existed for centuries in mountainous and northern regions, such as Turkey and Persia, where the rough climate means that long, thick fur is essential to a cat's survival in the wild.

The first longhaired cats in Europe arrived some time during the 16th century, probably via France from Ankara in Turkey (then known as Angora). Initially they were referred to as French cats, later to be known as Angoras. They were followed by other longhaired cats brought into Europe from Persia, although it is not known whether this was their place of origin. The cats from Persia differed from those from Turkey, having broader heads with smaller ears and shorter noses. Their fur, too, was of a different texture, being longer and thicker.

A man named Harrison Weir (1824-1905), known as "the Father of the Cat Fancy", was the first person to organise cat shows in Britain. A Fellow of the Horticultural Society and a leading authority on poultry breeding and showing, he was also a cat illustrator and author of the book *Our Cats*. Feeling that the domestic cat was neglected and generally regarded with contempt, Weir decided to foster a wider appreciation of the animal by organising cat shows. He devised the schedule for the world's first cat show, held at London's Crystal Palace in July 1871. He also devised the very first "points of excellence" (later to become the "standard of points") as guidelines for the appearance of each cat breed. This was used at the Crystal Palace show and at many subsequent shows, including the first American cat show in New York in 1895. Even today many standards have his points of excellence as a base.

Harrison Weir described the ideal longhaired cat as having a rather short nose with a round, broad head. Because of his description, breeders aimed for this type, and eventually the Angora, more slender and with a longer face, disappeared altogether. In 1903 Miss Frances Simpson, a cat judge, admitted she had never been able to distinguish between the Angora and the Persian cat (there had been extensive interbreeding), and she considered all longhaired cats to be Persian. The Angora was not re-introduced to Britain until the 1950s, when some specimens were imported from Turkey.

Persians are now officially known as Longhairs, or Persian-type Longhairs, in Britain. Other longhaired breeds, such as the Angora or Birman, are referred to as semi-longhair. However, the breed is still officially named "Persian" in most other countries, and in Britain this is what the cats are called in everyday language.

Those very early Persian cats differed considerably from the Persian of today. They had longer faces, taller ears and shorter fur than their modern descendants, qualities that would today mark a "pet quality cat" (that is, one not up to show standard). Selective breeding has changed the appearance of the Persian drastically over the years; the face is much shorter, the body lower and the fur longer. In some cases, breeding has been taken to the extreme, and the result is the so-called Ultra-type Persian. These are extremely flat-faced cats, with the cat's nose at the same level as its eyes. Ultra-type Persians are very common in America and on the continent, where they often gain top honours at shows. However, the GCCF believes that Ultra is not the type to aim for, and so most Persian standards of points list it as a withholding fault "if the upper edge of the nose leather is above the lower edge of the eye", which means that judges are not allowed to award certificates to such cats. This ruling has caused a lot of controversy, as some breeders (and judges) like this type of cat and want to be able to show it. But it is questionable how healthy such a cat can be when the face is so very flat.

the persian as a pet

2

Persians and Exotics make ideal companions for children as they are so placid and good tempered. The author's two year old daughter Rebecca has enjoyed the company of Persians all her life. Photo - Shaun Flannery.

The Persian cat can be an ideal pet, but it may not necessarily be yours! You should think carefully and do your homework thoroughly before deciding what breed of cat to buy. Check on the characteristics of different breeds, read cat books, visit cat shows, and talk to cat breeders.

The Persian is usually a very friendly and laid-back type of cat. Unlike the Siamese, it is not very noisy, and it is not particularly likely to wreck your house, although this has been known! The calm, easy-going nature of the Persian makes it an ideal cat for those who do not want an extrovert, and it is certainly a breed which likes to spend time purring on its owner's lap.

Self-coloured Persians, such as the Cream, tend to be the calmest of the varieties. At the other end of the scale is the Colourpoint, perhaps because this was originally bred from a cross between a Persian and a Siamese. However, just because Persians are laid-back, do not think they are boring! They are still playful and lots of fun.

Having considered the Persian's temperament, the next thing to consider is its coat. A Persian cat will need grooming several times a week, every week of its life. A Persian with a neglected coat is a very sorry sight, and usually a very sad cat; it is quite amazing how quickly fur can mat if it is not groomed regularly. If you are going to own a Persian, you must be prepared to groom your cat. It is very easy to fall for that fluffy little chocolate-box kitten, but the kitten will grow up into a big cat with a good deal more fur. It is cruel not to groom a Persian regularly, as selective breeding has left the cat helpless without you.

Creme and white Bi-colour Persian. This beautiful coat needs a lot of attention and must be groomed several times a week. Photo - Jeff Spall.

Most Persians will not object to grooming once they are accustomed to it, but there are some who genuinely do not like it. If yours does object, you must remember that it would be far more unfair to give up than to persevere with the grooming, however unpleasant. It is not uncommon for Persians to be taken to the veterinary surgery with fur so badly neglected that a general anaesthetic has to be administered before the mats can be removed! If you are still interested in owning a Persian but balk at the idea of all that grooming, there is an excellent alternative: the Exotic Shorthair cat is a Persian in all respects bar one - it has a short coat! The result of selective breeding between Longhairs and British Shorthairs, the

The result of a badly neglected coat. This Persian had to have his sides and tummy shaved under general anaesthetic, as his fur was so badly matted.
Photo - Shaun Flannery.

13

Persian Cats

Exotic is available in all the Persian colour combinations, and combines the calm, affectionate nature of the Persian with the more alert, outgoing temperament of its other ancestor.

A Persian cat will also need bathing from time to time, something which is not usually necessary for shorthaired cats. If it has an upset stomach, its fur is likely to become very soiled, and the cat will need help to clean itself.

A Persian's eyes are often naturally runny (see chapter 6) and the area underneath the eyes must be wiped clean. In short, a Persian cat needs care and attention, so do not expect it to be as independent as other cats.

The perfect answer for the Persian lover who cannot cope with the demands of a longhaired cat. The Exotic is essentially a Persian cat with short fur. This Shaded Silver queen goes by the name of Hilal Katy, and belongs to the author.
Photo - Shaun Flannery.

Because of its long fur, the Persian cat is not really an outdoor cat. If it is allowed to roam free, its fur will very quickly get dirty and matted. It is far better to give the cat an enclosed outdoor run, or not to let it out at all.

This is not cruel, as so many people seem to think. Persian cats have been bred indoors for generations, and there is hardly any vestige left in them of the instinct to go out and hunt, still so strong in many breeds. A Persian will be perfectly happy to spend all its life indoors, and this trait makes the breed ideal for flat-dwellers or people living near a busy road, who would find it difficult to keep a cat that needed to go outside regularly.

The Shorthaired version of the Blue Persian: the Blue Exotic. Photo - Jeff Spall.

buying a

persian

3

Where do I find my Persian ?

The simple answer to this question is "... from a reputable breeder". If you take the time to find a good, caring breeder, it is likely to pay off in years to come. You can find a good, pet quality Persian kitten by scanning the advertisements in your local paper, but you may also end up with a sickly kitten from a "backstreet breeder" who is in it purely for the money. Similarly, pet

shops sell kittens to make money. A pedigree kitten bought from a pet shop is likely to cost more than if it were bought directly from its breeder, and you are unlikely to get the same guarantees that the shop-bought kitten has been brought up properly.

A good breeder is one who cares for his (or her) cats. They will ideally be living indoors, but, if they are outside, they should be housed in purpose-built cat houses. It is important to bear in mind that kittens brought up as part of the family are more likely to adapt easily to normal family life. Many advertisements do give an indication as to whether kittens are used to children and/or dogs. A caring breeder will have done everything he or she can to make sure that the kittens have had a good start in life.

Red Tabby Persian kitten.
Photo - Isabelle Francais.

He will have spent time with the kittens every day, getting them used to being handled and groomed. He will have fed them the best possible diet, and made sure that they are healthy. Very importantly, he will not sell his kittens until they are at least 12 weeks old. Forget everything you have heard about kittens being able to leave their mother between six and eight weeks of age: they are not! Persian kittens will often suckle their mother for up to ten weeks, and the GCCF recommends that no kitten should be sold before the age of 12 weeks. A kitten of that age should be fully weaned, toilet trained, and immunised. The GCCF holds details of various cat clubs which in turn will often be able to recommend good breeders. Many clubs also have kitten lists, detailing kittens currently available. Another excellent way to find a kitten is to check advertisements and breeders' registers in the various cat magazines. Be prepared to wait for the right kitten. Breeders find it very annoying to have enquiries from people who are not prepared to wait until the kittens reach the age of 12 weeks. Impatience does not pay off - what you want is worth waiting for.

Finally, do not neglect the various breed rescue societies, cat shelters like the Cats Protection League, and the RSPCA. Persian cats are often abandoned because owners feel unable to cope with the amount of grooming required. If you do not mind taking on an adult cat with an unknown pedigree, you will be doing a really good deed in rescuing a previously unwanted animal.

Kitten or Adult ?

I have already mentioned that a kitten should be at least 12 weeks old before it comes to live with you. A kitten of this age can be a real joy, with all its antics and games. Buying a young kitten is always the easiest option, offering you the chance to shape your cat. You will be able to introduce it to all aspects of life: being groomed, being taken to the vet, where to go to the toilet. That is not to say that an adult cat will not make a good pet. It probably will, but it may take just a little longer to settle in its new home. If you already own a cat or a dog, it is advisable to buy a kitten rather than an adult cat. Established pets will accept a kitten much more easily than they would an adult.

Persian Cats

Male or Female ?

Should you buy a male or female cat? Well, this really comes down to personal preference. If you want your cat for breeding purposes, you will have specific requirements, but if you want a cat purely as a pet or a show cat (or both) and do not wish to breed from it, the choice between the sexes is less important, as both males and females make excellent pets. Male cats are usually larger than females, and in my experience Persian males tend to remain more playful and kitten-like in later life. On the other hand, a female may be slightly more affectionate. Very often the breeder may only have one sex available. You should not be put off by this, even if you had set your heart on the opposite, as I am sure that you will be just as pleased with either.

One or Two Cats ?

Should you stick with one kitten, or plump for more? It rather depends on how much time you want to spend on your cat. A single cat will be happy if it gets a great deal of attention from you, and is not left alone for long periods during the day. However, I have found that single cats often become very "humanized", developing habits not found in cats who enjoy more feline company. Many single cats tend to be fussy eaters, perhaps because they have no competition. They may also be less playful than a cat with a constant sparring partner. It is perfectly possible to have a happy single cat. But if you are out at work, do consider buying two cats. They will be friends for life, and will benefit from each other's company. They will never be lonely, as there will always be a friend nearby, and will have lots of fun . There are very few sights as lovely as two kittens playing together. A pair of cats will not be any less affectionate towards their owner than a single cat; merely slightly less dependent on you.

Pet Quality, Breeding Quality, or Show Quality ?

For the novice pedigree cat owner, some advertisements may seem very confusing. They may talk about kittens being "pet quality", "show quality", or "breeding quality". Other terms, including "show/neuter" are common as well. What does it all mean, and what should you choose?

It is all very simple, really. A pet quality cat is a cat which is just that: a pet. It is still a purebred pedigree cat, but it is not suitable either for showing or for breeding.

It will have one or more faults rendering it useless at shows, and unsuitable for breeding, but these faults will be purely cosmetic. The cat will be no less qualified to make a lovely pet. Common faults in pet quality Persians include too long a face, tail defects such as a slight kink at the tip, or perhaps a very undershot bite. None of these "defects" will make the slightest difference to a prospective owner who wants his cat as a pet.

The Colourpoint colouring can also be combined with the Tabby gene. This is Seal Tabby Colourpoint Blondbella Chiquita, bred and owned by the author.
Photo - Shaun Flannery.

Not all Persians are show quality. This is Blondie, the author's first Persian, and her face and legs are too long for her to compete at shows. However, such Persians can still make delightful pets.
Photo - Shaun Flannery.

Persian Cats

A breeding quality cat is always female. She is not quite good enough to show, but has no serious defects preventing her owner breeding from her. A female kitten with a slightly undershot jaw can still have lovely type and colour, and can produce kittens with good bites. Similarly, she may have a slight colour or marking fault, which would not necessarily be passed on to her kittens. A male cat advertised as a show neuter is deemed good enough to be on the show bench, but not quite good enough to be a stud. This cat should be neutered, but he can still be shown in the neuter classes. A stud cat must be of top quality, as he is likely to produce many more kittens than a queen.

A cat advertised as show quality (or show/stud, show/breeding) is suitable for all purposes. It has good showing potential (bearing in mind it is difficult to be certain about how a 12-week-old kitten will appear in adulthood) and will also be suitable for breeding. Of course, it will also make a nice pet, but most breeders prefer to sell their show prospects to owners keen to show their cats.

How Much will it Cost ?

What price should you expect to pay for your kitten? Well, that can vary tremendously. Firstly, how much you pay depends on what classification the kitten is given by its breeder. A pet quality kitten will be much cheaper than one classified as show quality. Prices also vary between breeds. In some breeds a show quality kitten might cost £250, whereas the same amount of money will buy you only a pet in a different breed. It is impossible to offer an accurate estimate in a book, as prices vary considerably from area to area, and from year to year. Generally speaking, at 1996 prices, you could expect to pay between £150 and £600 for a Persian kitten.

Documentation

When you buy a pedigree kitten, there are certain documents which you should receive from the breeder. Their exact nature depends on whether it is pet, breeding, or show quality.

A pet quality kitten may not be given anything other than a vaccination certificate, along with any information sheets the breeder has designed; a diet sheet, for example. Some breeders will give a pedigree, but not a registration certificate. Others will provide both a pedigree and a registration certificate. All pet quality kittens should have been registered on the GCCF's non-active register. This means the cat cannot officially be used for breeding. The breeder alone has the right to change a cat's registration from non-active to the active register. The cat can be shown, although there would not be much serious point in doing so, as the breeder probably had good reason to sell it as a pet. If the kitten is sold without any registration papers, but with a pedigree, the new owner can register the kitten himself, even against the wishes of the breeder. If he places it on the active register, he can breed from it. To prevent this happening, most breeders will either place their pet quality kittens on the non-active register, or decline to offer a pedigree. However, the provision of a pedigree is recommended.

All breeding quality and show quality cats should have a full set of papers, including pedigree, registration certificate and vaccination certificate. If you choose one of these cats, it is very important to check your kitten has been registered on the active register, or you will not be able to register any kittens bred from it. A kitten registered on the non-active register has the words "no progeny to be registered" written on its certificate. The registration certificate should have been signed on the reverse by the breeder, and you can transfer the cat's registration into your name. Details of how to do this can be found on the back of the registration certificate.

Many breeders will also give their kittens free insurance for the first six weeks in its new home. This could obviously be very advantageous should anything happen to the kitten.

Choosing a Kitten

Selecting your kitten from a whole litter can be a difficult job. You will usually find that not all the kittens are for sale, as breeders often wish to keep the best one for themselves, and, anyway, other prospective owners may have placed bookings ahead of you. If you are lucky enough actually to have a choice, there are several things you should consider.

If you are only after a kitten as a pet, you need not bother too much about appearance. They will all be cute! What matters more is that the kitten is healthy and in good condition, so check it very thoroughly.

Almost all Persian cats have runny eyes, so such a condition is not necessarily a sign of illness. But the eyes should be bright and clear, with no sign of redness or pus, any liquid being clear or slightly brown in colour. The nose must be clean; sneezing or snuffling could be a sign of cat flu.

The kitten's ears should also be clean. Many kittens suffer a build-up of wax in their ears, but this should not be too prominent and it should be possible to wipe away the wax easily. A kitten with a dark-coloured, crusty discharge in its ears is likely to have ear mites, although this is not very common in pedigree cats. (It is much more prevalent in outdoor cats.)

The kitten's bottom and surrounding fur should be clean. Many Persian kittens have rather delicate stomachs which will easily be upset, but no responsible breeder should sell a kitten suffering from an upset stomach until it has recovered. Do not expect the kitten to be sparkling clean, as Persian kittens have an incredible knack for getting dirty. However, there is a limit: the fur should appear well looked-after, and should be free from knots, indicating that the kitten has been regularly groomed. It should also be free of fleas.

The kitten should be neither too thin nor too fat: a very fat kitten with a "pot belly" may have worms. Finally, the kitten should be alert and playful when awake, and should not run away from you once it has conquered its initial shyness. Any responsible cat breeder will have their cats tested for Feline Leukaemia Virus (FeLV) before mating; sometimes the tests will extend to other diseases, such as Feline Immunodeficiency Virus (FIV). It may be worth asking to see the parents' certificates to ensure as far as possible that the kitten is in top health.

American style Chinchillas, like this 12-week-old kitten, have a slightly darker colouring and a more luxurious coat than their British counterparts. Photo - Jeff Spall.

If you are in search of a show quality kitten, you will need to be even more thorough when making your choice. Most breeders are honest and will explain each kitten's good and bad points, but do bear in mind that it can be difficult to tell how a young kitten will shape up as an adult. The contours of its face may change slightly for example; the bite may change as its permanent teeth appear; its colour and coat may change. A very promising kitten can usually be spotted at an early age, but do not blame the breeder if as an adult your kitten does not fulfil its promise. Much depends on you, its new owner. It is important that the kitten is reared correctly. When picking a show kitten, you should select one with a nice round head and a short nose with a good break above it. (See Show Standards in Chapter 8.) The bite should be even, not undershot. The ears should be small, well-spaced and rounded. The eyes should be large and round, and of the colour appropriate to that particular variety.

The legs should be short and stocky, the tail short and even with no kink, dent or bump. Finally, the cat's overall colour should conform to the standard of points for the variety.

If you have chosen your kitten before it is ready to leave for its new home, you are very likely to be asked to pay a non-returnable deposit, usually between 10 and 20% of its total price. Do not expect your breeder to reserve a kitten for you without such a deposit: people often change their minds, and the breeder will not want to risk being left with an unsold kitten, having turned away other prospective buyers. A deposit makes the deal more secure for both parties.

Bringing a New Kitten Home

Once your chosen kitten is 12 weeks old and fully vaccinated, you will be able to bring it home. Make sure you have a secure travelling box in which to transport the kitten (see Chapter 4). A cardboard box or carrier is not sufficient to withstand a frightened kitten capable of tearing its way out. Travelling should not be a completely new experience for your kitten however, as it is likely to have made at least two trips to the vet for inoculations.

Upon arriving home with your kitten, release it from the box and allow it plenty of time to explore its new home. Just leave it alone as much as possible, giving it a chance to sniff around, but keep a watchful

The kittens are now 12 weeks old, fully weaned and ready to leave for their new homes. Photo - Shaun Flannery.

eye on things so the newcomer does not stumble into some sort of trouble. Some kittens may prefer to stay in one room for the first couple of days, until they feel brave enough to venture further. Make sure your kitten knows where food and water or milk are served, and show it where to find the litter tray. It will not usually take a new arrival long to settle in; your kitten will soon seem very much at home.

This settling-in process may take a little longer if you already have other cats, or a dog. Nearly all cats will accept a kitten, but it often takes them a few days to do so. Keep a close eye on what is going on. The older cat is quite likely to hiss at the newcomer, and may also hit out at it if the kitten comes too close. Just ignore this, as long as the "attack" is not too bad; most kittens will not take offence. But it would be wise to separate them at times when you are unable to supervise them, such as at night. In this way you will be sure no real harm comes to the kitten. If you just let things take their course the older cat will probably soon be playing with its new friend.

Just one word of advice: do not make too much of a fuss over the kitten in front of the established cat, as this is likely to make the older cat feel left out. Remember to show your older cat lots of affection, reminding him he is still "number one" and that his position in your household is not threatened.

Introducing a kitten to a dog may be more difficult - progress will largely depend on the dog. Most dogs will accept a kitten without too many problems. Let the dog and cat get acquainted carefully, but remember the kitten may be frightened at first. It is wise to keep the dog in a separate room until the kitten has got used to the idea. If the dog is very excitable, it may also be best to keep him on a lead when he meets the kitten for the very first time. In my experience as an owner of 15 cats and four dogs, the two species can get on very well. Very often I find one or two cats sleeping next to a dog in the dog's bed. In fact the strong friendships that do develop between dogs and cats are quite surprising when you take into account a quite distinct language barrier! Wagging a tail signifies friendliness in a dog, but means something entirely different when performed by a cat, usually indicating anger or insecurity.

If you have children by all means let them handle the new kitten, but do make sure they take care, and ensure they leave the kitten alone after a while. It will tire quickly and need to sleep.

Finally

So now you have your Persian kitten: the pet of your dreams. Remember that you are responsible for the cat's well-being for the rest of its life. A Persian cat can live for 15 years or more, and it is not a pet to be discarded once the novelty has worn off. You must make sure your cat is always well fed, well groomed, and in good health. You should take your Persian to the vet each year to be inoculated, as well as when it appears unwell. If it is a pet, and not a breeding cat, you should also have it neutered. When you go on holiday, you must make sure the cat is properly looked after if you are unable to take it with you. All this is part of being a responsible cat owner; it is well to consider everything before buying your Persian.

Children love animals and will enjoy helping to care for them, but remember that the ultimate responsibility for household pets lies with adult owners. Young children cannot be expected to remember to feed and care for a pet properly, no matter how many promises have been made.

general care 4
& equipment

How do I look after my Persian cat, and what equipment will I need? Over the years, a good variety of equipment has become available to cat owners in pet shops, and Persian owners will find much of it useful. Many cats live quite happily without much grooming or pampering, but your Persian will be more dependent on you, so good equipment is essential.

Litter Trays

The first absolute essential for your Persian cat is a litter tray. Assuming your cat will spend its life indoors, an indoor toilet is a must; even if your cat is allowed outside, a litter tray can be useful for night-time and other occasional use. The litter tray should be of a good size, and as deep as possible. The hooded type is usually the best, as cats like to have some privacy when going to the toilet. There are many good types of litter tray currently available in pet shops. If you only have one cat, one litter tray will usually be enough, although the cat might like an extra one if you live in a house on two or more storeys. If you have more than one cat, you will need more than one litter tray. Cats are usually very clean animals, and do not like to use dirty litter trays. The litter tray should be situated in a quiet corner, perhaps in the bathroom. It is not usually a good idea to place the litter tray close to where people eat, as you will want to avoid unpleasant odours at meal times.

There is also a variety of cat litters from which to choose. Most of these are very good, and it is usually simply a case of trial and error to discover which type best suits you and your cat.

Kittens will learn to use a litter tray by copying their mother.
Photo - Vincent Serbin.

There are many types of litter tray available. This is a hooded one, which gives the cat some privacy, together with a lipped type, which is designed to prevent the cat litter from being kicked out.
Photo - Shaun Flannery.

Generally speaking, white litters should be avoided as they are often rather dusty, and can cause irritation to a Persian's sensitive eyes. Wood-based cat litters are usually very good, but I have found that as the pellets disintegrate once they are wet, the sawdust often clings to the fur of a longhaired cat. It is not advisable to use anything other than cat litter in your cat's litter tray. Newspaper or tissue will get very wet and smelly, and the cat will not be able to dig in it. Sawdust or wood shavings are completely unsuitable as not only will they cling to a Persian's fur and so be distributed throughout the house, but they will also fail to mask unpleasant smells adequately.

The litter tray will require cleaning out from time to time. Many cat litters will become lumpy when wet. These lumps can easily be removed, along with any faeces, and a small amount of new litter can be added. In this way, the tray can be kept clean, and will only need a thorough cleaning and washing once a week or so. If you have more than one cat it is more difficult to keep the tray clean, so the whole tray should be cleaned out as soon as it appears dirty. Few cats like to use a dirty litter tray, and if it is not regularly cleaned your cat is likely to look for somewhere else to go to toilet.

Food and Water Bowls

The next essential items on your shopping list are two bowls: one for food and one for water or milk. Your cat should always have access to a drink. There are many different bowls available in pet shops, and most will serve their purpose quite adequately, but you will probably find a metallic bowl the most practical. These can be cleaned easily, and are unlikely to break if dropped on the floor.

By far the best type of food bowl is a metal one, which is easy to clean and unbreakable. Photo - Shaun Flannery.

Find a quiet spot in the kitchen to feed your cat, in a corner, or under or on a work surface. Cats like to pick out pieces of their food when they eat, placing them next to their bowl, so bear this in mind when choosing your spot: the area should be easy to keep clean.

If you have more than one cat, you should provide a food bowl for each of them. It is not fair to expect more than one cat to feed from a single large bowl, as cats eat at different speeds, and a slower eater may be rushed unnecessarily, or find itself losing its lunch to a rival diner!

The automatic cat feeders now available in many pet shops are specially designed contraptions which, with the help of a timing device, allow you to feed your cat when you are away. They can be very useful, but do bear in mind that each feeder will only feed one cat. Shop around carefully before you purchase one, as some of the cheaper models can be broken into by a clever cat, and then the whole point of the exercise is lost!

Travelling Box

This is also an essential item as there are certain to be times when you need to transport your cat safely, be it to a cat show, from the breeder, to a stud for mating, or just to the vet for its annual jabs. A simple cardboard box is not strong enough, and will not be secure.

Here again a great variety of travelling boxes and cages is available in pet shops. Most are very good, but avoid wicker carriers as they offer less security than plastic or wire containers.

An all-wire carrier with a lid can be very practical, and it is usually easy to get a cat in and out of it. Covered plastic carriers with a door at one end are more popular, as a cat is likely to feel more secure inside, and be warmer on a cold day, but the task of getting a cat in and out may be slightly more difficult.

A carrying box is essential when transporting a cat. Most cats prefer this covered type, which gives them a sense of security.
Photo - Shaun Flannery.

Get your kitten used to its carrier right from the start. Do not just use it for unpleasant trips like visiting the vet. Leave the carrier standing open in a room for a while so that your kitten can play inside it, and learn that there is nothing to fear. A cat who gets used to travelling at an early age is unlikely to present a problem in later life.

Cat Beds

Does your cat need a special bed? The answer to this is no. Most cats will choose their own special resting place; it will very often be your favourite armchair, or perhaps your bed. Many cats also like to sleep on window sills, tables, or simply on the floor. It is impossible to tell a cat it is not allowed to sleep in a particular place. If you do not want it in your bed the only answer is to close the bedroom door. If you wish to pamper your pet, however, there is no reason why you should not buy him a special cat bed.

There are many types to choose from, and most cats love them. Do not expect them to forsake other favoured resting places: they will only sleep in their customised bed when they feel like it!

A soft bed like this will make an ideal resting place for your Persian, or he may just prefer to choose his own napping spot.
Photo - Shaun Flannery.

Collars

Indoor cats are unlikely to need collars, and if you are planning to show your Persian you must not use one as it will wear away your cat's coat around the neck. If you allow your cat outside, however, it ought to wear a collar for its own safety, in case it gets lost. I find it useful to put collars on all my non-show cats even if they are not strictly allowed out, as it is possible a cat may get out by mistake; once it is lost, a collar and disc will give it a much better chance of being returned safe and sound.

For safety reasons a cat collar should be partly elasticated. Cats hide in bushes and climb trees, and the collar may easily get caught on a twig or branch. If it is partly elasticated, it will be possible for the collar to slip over the cat's head, leaving the animal free to escape; if not, the cat will be trapped.

I prefer ordinary collars to flea collars for my cats. Some cats are allergic to flea collars, and may lose the fur underneath the collar or develop a reddening of the skin next to it. If you do decide to use a flea collar, check your cat for adverse reactions after a day or two.

Grooming Equipment

This will be dealt with much more thoroughly in Chapter 6. To summarise: you will need three or four different metal combs, and perhaps a brush as well. You will need one wide-toothed comb, one moulting comb (with teeth of varying lengths), one very fine comb, and one flea comb. The brush can be either a "Slicker Brush" or an ordinary brush.

Scratching Posts

A scratching post is a very useful piece of equipment, especially if purchased when the cat is still a young kitten. A kitten who has become used to a scratching post at an early age is less likely to ruin your furniture with its claws later on. Scratching posts come in many shapes and sizes, and can cost anything from a couple of pounds to hundreds! Most will have been treated with cat nip, a herb which smells very attractive to cats and is used to draw the cat's attention to the scratching post. Posts in the shape of cat "trees" are very good. Made of wood, they are covered in carpeting, and usually feature a post with one or more shelves for the cat to sit on. The more interesting the scratching post, the more likely your cat is to use it.

In Britain, de-clawing of cats has been outlawed: the practice is rightly condemned as very cruel. Vets will not perform such an operation, and a de-clawed cat cannot be exhibited at any UK shows.

A scratching post is a must if your furniture is going to stay intact ! There are hundreds of models to choose from. Always introduce your Persian to his scratching post as a young kitten, before he has decided that your favourite armchair is his favourite scratching place.
Photo - Shaun Flannery.

A cat needs its claws for a variety of purposes. They are essential for climbing, jumping and balancing; they are used for defence; and a kitten will "knead" the mother's teats with its claws to make her milk flow. A cat without claws is a severely handicapped cat.

Toys

Pet shops have a vast array of cat toys available. Most cats love to play, and I have yet to meet a cat owner who has not fallen prey to the temptation to buy toys for his or her pet. A cat can manage very well without special toys, however, playing instead with whatever is available, such as a screwed-up piece of paper or a pine cone. If you do decide to buy your cat some toys, choose items without small parts which may come off. Animals' toys are not covered by the same safety standards as children's toys, so they can sometimes be dangerous. Check carefully that small parts are not likely to fall off or be swallowed accidentally.

Caring for your Cat's Eyes

Use a soft cloth or special eye wipe to wipe away the discharge around your Persian's eyes.
Photo - Isabelle Francais.

Most Persian cats have naturally runny eyes. The extent to which your cat's eyes are affected will depend on the flatness of its face: in an extremely flat-faced cat, the tear ducts may be slightly squashed. This condition is nothing to worry about; as long as the discharge from the eyes is not pus-like (yellow or green), and as long as the eyes and eyelids are not red and swollen, the cat is fine. It will need help to clean beneath its eyes, however. On a dark cat, tear stains will not show very much, but on a white or cream cat, the staining will become very obvious and may be difficult to remove if it is allowed to get too bad, and a white cat with brown "gutters" is not a pretty sight. Remedies are available which will bleach away such marks, but it is better to prevent them in the first place.

When the eyes have "overflowed", gently wipe away all the discharge below, being careful not to touch the eye itself. Quite often you will find you need to do this after the cat has eaten. Use a ball of damp cotton wool, or a special eye wipe available from pet shops. Because of the close connection, your cat's nostrils will often need slight attention as well.

Caring for your Cat's Ears

A healthy ear will not normally need cleaning, but Persians often suffer slightly from a build-up of wax. If this happens, wipe the excess away from the outer ear with a ball of damp, perhaps slightly soapy, cotton wool, but do not probe into the ear itself. The area should then be patted dry with clean cotton wool.

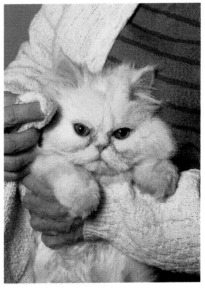

Only use a cotton top to clean out your Persian's ear if it is excessively dirty.
Photo - Isabelle Francais.

Normally, any dirt and wax inside the ear can easily be wiped away with a soft cloth.
Photo - Isabelle Francais.

Caring for your Cat's Teeth

Any pet cat's teeth will eventually become covered in tartar. This is inevitable, and any amount of hard, crunchy food given does not seem to make a great deal of difference. The problem is likely to begin slowly as the cat reaches one year of age, starting with a slight build-up of tartar, and in order to protect the teeth, prevention is better than cure.

If you can get one, gently use a dentist's tooth scraper to scrape away any tartar as soon as it appears. If you begin at an early age, the cat will probably not mind too much. Continue regularly, and hopefully you will be able to avoid visiting the vet to have your cat's teeth de-scaled.

However, if tartar is allowed to build up, tooth decay can set in. Any heavy build-up of tartar must therefore be removed by a vet. This is usually done under anaesthetic. Although incidents of cats reacting badly to the anaesthetic, sometimes fatally, are uncommon, it is far better if you can remove tartar yourself as it appears rather than let it accumulate.

Caring for your Cat's Claws

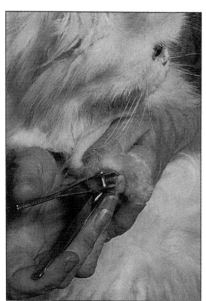

A cat which has access to a good scratching post will not usually need any special attention to its claws. However, if you wish to show your cat it is advisable to trim its claws, especially on its front paws, just before the show. Use a pair of nail scissors, and cut off the tip of the claw to blunt it, reducing the likelihood of the cat scratching anyone by mistake. The sharp tip will grow out again in a few days.

Trimming of the claws is sometimes necessary, especially before a show. Only the very tip of each claw should be cut off. Photo - Isabelle Francais.

Worming your Cat

An indoor cat is unlikely to get worms, but it will not be completely immune. Your cat should be wormed regularly at least every six months, while a cat which is allowed out will need worming every three months.

You can buy worming pills from vets, pharmacists, or pet shops. There are two different groups: one kills roundworms, the other attacks tapeworms. Roundworms are the most common type of worms afflicting cats: treatment should be given in two stages, a second dose being administered two weeks after the first to kill any eggs which may have hatched in the cat's stomach. During the week between doses, a single tapeworm treatment can be given. Although the tapeworm treatment might make the cat vomit, this is not serious and is no cause for alarm. Most treatments take the form of a pill, but roundworm treatment is also available in liquid form to cater for difficult patients. It is now also possible to buy a single-dose tablet which will treat both types of worm.

The best way to administer a pill to a cat is to sit the animal firmly on a table. Carefully open its mouth, then simply pop the pill into the back of the mouth, on its tongue. Close its mouth and hold it closed until the cat swallows. This will, however, require some practice, and it may be a good idea to ask your vet for a demonstration.

Alternatively, crush the pill in some of your cat's favourite food, and hope he will not notice he is eating it. Bear in mind, however, that this method is less reliable, as your cat may leave some or all of its food.

Fleas

Even the cleanest cat living in the cleanest house is likely at some stage to suffer from fleas, and most cats will need regular treatment against fleas. I have covered this topic more extensively in the chapter on health and diseases.

Inoculations

Your cat will need booster vaccinations once a year, having previously received two initial inoculations, usually administered before the kitten leaves its mother, at the ages of nine and 12 weeks.

There are a few diseases which should always be vaccinated against: Feline Panleucopaenia (infectious enteritis); and two types of "cat 'flu" - Feline Viral Rhinotracheitis and Feline Calici Virus.

All cats are at risk from these deadly diseases, whether or not they venture outdoors; for this reason annual booster injections are essential.

In recent years it has become possible to vaccinate against two additional diseases, Feline Leukaemia Virus and Feline Chlamydia. These vaccines are not given routinely, but if you are worried, it is as well to consult your vet on the matter.

Neutering

Any cat you do not intend to use for breeding should be neutered. The process is very simple for male cats and only slightly more complicated for females. Your vet will be able to advise you when you should have the operation performed. It is usually done when the cat is about six months old.

A cat that has not been neutered will not make a very good pet, and will become a nuisance. Eventually a tom cat will start to "spray" urine all over its living quarters (your house!) in a bid to mark out his territory. The only way to stop or prevent this instinctive behaviour is have him neutered.

In adulthood, an entire queen will come into season, "calling" and sometimes spraying at regular intervals, perhaps as often as every week. She will call loudly, and her mind will be totally focused on sex and kittens; she is likely to go off her food. A cat which is allowed to call indefinitely is likely eventually to develop cysts on her fallopian tubes.

Un-neutered cats are very likely to attempt escapes from the house in search of a mate, and a tom cat will probably get into fights. If you do not intend to allow your cat to fulfil its natural sexual instincts by mating and breeding, it is fairer to have it neutered and avoid its inevitable frustration. Neutered cats are happy cats, and are very friendly.

Going on Holiday

If you are going on holiday and are not able to bring your cat with you, alternative arrangements must be made. Perhaps a friend could stay at your house, or pop round each day. Sending the cat to stay at a boarding cattery is a widely-used solution, and details of nearby catteries can be found in the telephone directory. Before you make a definite booking, make sure you visit the premises: you should look for cleanliness, security, and caring staff who will look after your cat.

A good boarding cattery will have large indoor areas which can be heated during the winter, with connecting outdoor runs. There should be a safety corridor around the perimeter, so that if a cat does escape it cannot leave the cattery premises. Staff should be prepared to feed the cats on the food to which they are already accustomed (most good catteries stock a wide variety of food-stuffs) and the cattery proprietor should insist on seeing your cat's vaccination certificate.

feeding your persian cat 5

Feeding a cat or kitten is much more complicated than at first it may appear, as cats have unique and very specific nutritional requirements. They are obligate carnivores: they need to eat meat and cannot survive on a low-protein or vegetarian diet (unlike dogs who are omnivores and can live on a meat-free diet). An adult cat needs twice as much protein as a dog would require, and growing kittens need twice as much again.

Today there is a great variety of complete cat foods available in the shops; many are good, but some are not. In the past, when most pets survived principally on table scraps, cats supplemented their diets by hunting and catching mice, rats and birds. Now that many cats are kept indoors, and outdoor access is restricted, it is absolutely essential that you provide a good, balanced diet for your cat.

The feline intestine is adapted for a diet high in fat and protein, providing energy without excessive bulk. Proteins are essential for tissue-building, resistance to disease, good coat growth, and maintenance of muscles and bones. There are certain essential nutrients which cats, unlike dogs, do not produce for themselves, and it is therefore vital to ensure that these are present in the cat's diet.

Proteins are made up of amino acids, and cats need as many as 20 different amino acids to enable them to manufacture the protein their bodies need. Of these essential amino acids, ten can be produced by the cat; the remainder must be ingested via its food. Among these, Taurine (an amino acid found only in animal tissue, ie meat) is crucial to feline health. A lack of Taurine in a cat's diet will result in a chronic Taurine deficiency, which in turn can lead to a variety of unpleasant conditions. The most notorious of these are blindness and brain damage, but other effects are heart troubles and reproductive problems including infertility, small litters, and ill-thriving kittens.

There are also some essential fatty acids (fats) which cats are unable to produce, so these too must be present in their diet. Fats are an alternative to protein as a source of energy and are important in the prevention and treatment of skin diseases. Of these essential fats, arachidonic acid is present only in animal fats.

Vitamin deficiencies also can cause serious problems. Vitamins A and E are needed to ensure the normal functioning of a cat's membranes, while vitamin B derivatives sustain many enzymes. Of these, vitamin A can be found only in animal tissue. Both the A and the B groups of vitamins can be found in high levels in liver, a widely-used ingredient in commercially produced cat food, and in this form it is safe for cats to eat. However, cats find fresh liver addictive, and its long-term use may result in health problems caused by vitamin A overload: the cat is slowly poisoned (vitamin A toxicity).

One B vitamin, Thiamine, is essential, as deficiency will lead to brain damage. Thiamine can be destroyed by heat and by acidity. The destructive enzyme Thiaminase is present in some types of raw fish, so it is important always to cook fish before feeding it to your cat.

Vitamin K is important for blood clotting, and vitamin D is involved in bone metabolism. A vitamin E deficiency can cause painful inflammations.

However, it should be noted that too much vitamin can sometimes be just as dangerous as too little. For example, an excess of vitamin A can cause painful bone problems, and too much vitamin D can weaken bones.

Cats do not need fibre as such, but a small amount in their diet can be useful, helping the cat to rid itself of fur-balls, and relieving constipation. Too much fibre will reduce the cat's ability to digest food resulting in intestinal water retention; liquids normally dealt with by the kidneys and disposed of as urine may become too concentrated, resulting in Feline Urological Syndrome (FUS), which is further explored in the chapter on ailments.

The cat has no specific need for carbohydrates, but they are present in some cat foods as cereal, a cheap and inferior energy source. Cereal and vegetable proteins lack certain amino acids needed by the cat.

The cat's absorption of minerals varies with the type of food it is given. A diet rich in fat will lead to a reduced absorption of calcium and trace elements; while too much calcium can retard a kitten's growth, and reduce the absorption of other elements, mainly phosphorus, zinc, copper and iron. Too much phosphorus can result in calcium deficiency and kidney problems, while too much magnesium may result in FUS and too much sodium can also lead to kidney problems. Diets with a high ash content should be avoided if your cats is prone to FUS.

Choosing Your Cat's Food

So, how should you go about choosing food for your cat? Well, it is not quite as difficult as the complex list of requirements may imply, as there are many excellent branded cat foods available. Your kitten's breeder should have supplied you with a diet sheet, explaining exactly what foods your kitten has been fed so far, and what it will need in the future. Follow the breeder's advice; he (or she) will have gained a lot of experience in feeding kittens and cats. Your vet should also prove a good source of advice.

The big question is whether to choose tinned food, a complete dried food, or both. Most cats are fed tinned food, and do very well on it; the main difference between tinned foods and dry foods is water content. A can of cat food contains at least 75% water, while dry food contains a maximum of about 12% water. Dry food is therefore usually more economical, and takes up less storage space. In addition, cats need to eat less of it in order to receive a healthy balanced diet. However, cats fed exclusively on dry food must take in plenty of water, so extra care is required to ensure they always have enough to drink.

Water is the cat's single most important nutrient. Without water, it will soon become dehydrated, and will die much sooner than if left without food. A cat which is fed tinned food will automatically take in water with its meal, and is very seldom seen to be thirsty, but fresh water should still be constantly available. For adult cats, water is far better than milk, which should be fed only to kittens and pregnant/lactating queens. Many adult cats, Persians in particular, are sensitive to milk and will quickly develop diarrhoea. However, special milks developed for kittens and adult cats are available in pet shops and supermarkets.

Most cats will show little preference between tinned and dry food, so one solution could be to feed tinned food, offering dry food as an occasional treat or extra supplement. Alternatively, you could buy one of the semi-moist foods currently available.

It is always a good idea to read the label displayed on the packaging: ingredients are listed in descending order of content by weight. Bear in mind that meat and meat derivatives contain water so are likely to be among the heavier ingredients; this can mean that ingredients such as cereals may appear lower down the list than meat products even if a cereal is the food's main ingredient by volume. The more specific a food label, the easier it is to decide on the quality of a particular food. The best foods are those containing a large amount of animal ingredients.

How Much to Feed

The amount of food a cat needs depends mainly on the quality of the food; you should feed more of a lower quality (cereal-based) food than of a higher quality (meat-based) food. The recommendations on the can or packet of food should be used as a guideline only, as all cats are individuals and will need different quantities of food.

An adult cat (nine months upwards) will require two meals a day, one in the morning and one in the evening. Many cats like to nibble during the day, making one meal last several hours. This should be discouraged if you are using tinned food, as it can go off if left uncovered at room temperature for any length of time, especially in hot weather. Try removing the cat's bowl as soon as it stops eating (whether or not any food has been left), and you should find that the cat soon learns to eat up all its food at one sitting. If you have more than one cat to feed, they are more likely to finish their food quickly, for fear of losing it to a hungry rival!

It is important not to spoil your cat. Many cats will develop a preference for one particular food and refuse to eat anything else. If you relent, and allow your cat to stick to its favourite, you will very soon have a spoilt and picky cat. This is not unusual; some cats demand a particular tinned brand, or a favoured flavour. Some owners end up feeding their cat only fresh fish, and sometimes even baby-food! This should be avoided at all costs. Not only can it lead to serious dietary deficiencies; it is also extremely annoying.

Remember: no healthy cat will starve itself to death. If your cat is hungry enough, it will eat whatever is on offer. Of course, it is best not to spoil your cat in the first place. Introduce a wide variety of foods when it is a kitten, and the problem should never arise. My own cats will eat absolutely anything given the chance - even vegetables.

Feeding Growing Kittens

Feeding a kitten is a very different matter from feeding a fully grown cat. A growing kitten uses up to three times the energy of an adult cat, so it is absolutely essential that growing kittens receive adequate nutrition if they are to have the best possible start in life.

Kittens have very small stomachs, therefore they must eat a good quality diet, high in protein and energy. If the food is of a poor quality, the kitten may be unable to eat enough to satisfy its growth needs. In such cases, kittens may develop a pot-bellied appearance, grow at a slow rate, sustain poor muscle and skeletal development, and have a reduced resistance to infection. It may also have digestive problems such as diarrhoea.

By far the best food for kittens is one which has been specially formulated for them. These can be found either in tinned or dried form, and are high in protein and fat, so that the kitten does not need to eat a great deal to receive all the energy it needs. As a supplement to solid food, a specially formulated milk should be given in place of water.

Between the ages of 12 weeks and about six months, kittens should be given at least four meals a day. Kittens between six and nine months should receive three meals a day; after the age of nine months, when a cat is deemed to have reached adulthood, two meals should be enough.

Remember: growing kittens should be allowed to eat as much as they want.

Cats with Special Dietary Needs

Pregnant or lactating queens will need more energy than other adult cats: you should increase their intake to three or four meals a day, and offer specialized cat milk as a drink.

Old and sick cats (those with kidney problems, for example) may need special diets, and you should discuss their individual needs with your vet. Most vets will sell foods specially manufactured for cats with specific dietary requirements.

Supplements and Treats

Most pet shops these days stock a bewildering array of vitamin and mineral supplements. A healthy adult cat receiving a good quality diet will not need any supplements, but extra vitamins and calcium can be a good idea for pregnant queens and young kittens. Ask your vet and your cat's breeder for advice, and always follow the instructions on the label, being careful not to overdose your cat.

Cat treats can also be found in abundance, but if you want to give your cat a treat, limit it to once or twice a week, and do not overdo it. Many cats put on weight easily, and you must keep a watchful eye to ensure yours does not become overweight. Consider the treats as part of your cat's main meals, and cut down accordingly on the amount of food you offer at meal times.

grooming 6
your
persian

Like it or not, Persian cats must be groomed several times a week - every week - all their lives!

Grooming your Persian is not something that you do once the fur has grown long enough, or when it begins to look matted. Grooming should start as soon as you bring your kitten home from the breeder, and a good breeder will already have started to get it used to being groomed. It does not matter that your kitten may not have a great deal of long fur; the idea is to help it accept the grooming ritual, and the longer this is left the more difficult it will be to groom your cat in later life.

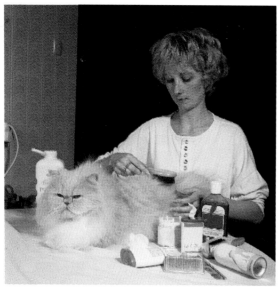

You will need a lot of equipment to prepare a Persian cat for a show.
Photo - Jeff Spall.

Essential Grooming Equipment

The following are essential items for grooming a Persian cat:

- A wide-toothed metal comb, available from pet shops.

- A moulting comb for cats: a metal comb with alternate long and short teeth, available in pet shops.

- A fine-toothed metal comb, available from pet shops.

- A flea comb: a very fine metal comb, available from pet shops.

- A specialised cat brush with fairly long bristles, available from pet shops.

- Baby talcum powder, available from a chemist.

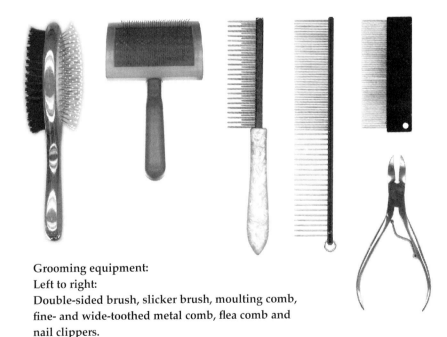

Grooming equipment:
Left to right:
Double-sided brush, slicker brush, moulting comb,
fine- and wide-toothed metal comb, flea comb and
nail clippers.

Normal Grooming

As a young kitten, your Persian will need very little grooming; a few minutes a day should be enough to get the kitten used to the process. Once the cat is older, you may find that grooming two or three times a week is about right, depending on the nature of its fur.

Using the fine metal comb, gently pull through the kitten's fur, talking reassuringly all the time. Let your kitten sniff the comb if he is interested, so that he knows there is nothing to fear. Comb through the fur on its back and tail first, then gently turn the kitten over on your lap and comb its stomach. This is really all you need do with young kittens. Most will try to bite the comb and make a game out of the whole affair! Once the fur starts to grow really long, you will need to groom the whole body more thoroughly, but until then, a token effort will suffice. While you are grooming, get into the habit of checking your cat's ears and looking inside them, and opening his mouth to examine his teeth. A cat who gets used to being handled in this way from an early age will usually be very easy to handle as an adult.

Grooming an adult cat in full coat is much more complicated. The amount of grooming needed by the cat will depend on the type of coat it carries. Not all Persians have the same fur: it can vary tremendously, even between closely related individuals. It may be easier to explain what I mean using the example of my own cats to illustrate some of the differences.

Blondie is a Cream Colourpoint, a neutered female. She has a fairly average coat, not very long. She needs grooming about once a week: if left any longer, her coat will start to knot. At first the knots will appear behind her ears, on the "ruff" (the fur on the chest) and on her stomach; if she is not combed at this stage, more knots will appear all over her body. Approximately every six months Blondie's coat will gradually become slightly greasy and at this time large areas of her fur will become matted. This calls for a thorough combing followed by a bath to remove the excess grease. Her coat should remain in good condition for the next six months, knot-free, if groomed regularly.

Endora is a Blue Cream Colourpoint, also a neutered female, and she is Blondie's granddaughter. In her full coat, Endora is a very striking cat, but her fur can be something of a nightmare. Her coat is very long and full, with a large ruff and a well-furnished tail. It is also very dense and soft, almost like cotton wool. Endora needs grooming every day to prevent her coat matting everywhere. Should this happen, it would take hours of work to untangle the fur! In addition she needs bathing regularly, every other month or so, to remove excess grease.

Cressi is a very easy cat. She is a Sealpoint Colourpoint queen, with a coat longer than Blondie's yet shorter than Endora's. Cressi's coat hardly ever gets knotted: I only need to give her a quick groom once a week and she never looks untidy. However, Cressi is one of my show cats, so she is bathed and powdered regularly, and receives intensive grooming for about a week before a show. If I kept her simply as a pet, her coat would be very little problem - she is the ideal pet Persian.

As you can see, the coats of Persians vary a great deal. In many cases you probably cannot predict exactly how your kitten's coat will develop, and neither can you rely on a kitten growing up to look like either of its parents. The best approach is to groom your Persian cat on the assumption that its coat needs a lot of attention, like that of Endora's. Once it is fully grown, you can experiment, gradually reducing the amount of grooming to establish the pattern that best suits your cat's coat.

However often you groom your Persian, your routine should be similar to this:

- Place your cat standing on a table for most of the grooming routine. However, when combing the stomach you will need to sit down with the cat laying on its back in your lap.
- Start by combing the whole cat (back, chest, tail, tummy and the "trousers" on its hind legs) using either a wide-toothed metal comb or a moulting comb. If the comb you have chosen moves through the fur easily, swap it for a fine-toothed comb. Work your way through the coat thoroughly, being careful not to miss any small knots. If you do find knots, gently tease them out with the comb, taking care not to hurt the cat. Knots often form behind the cat's front legs, on its stomach and in its trousers.
- If the coat feels greasy, apply powder: gently dust it with unperfumed talcum powder, then rub the powder into the fur. You can leave the powder in the coat to be combed out at the next grooming, but remember never to leave any powder in the cat's coat if you are taking it to a show: if you do, your cat will be disqualified immediately. It is important always to use unperfumed talcum powder (baby talc is best) because perfumed talcum powder is likely to irritate the cat's eyes.

Once you have finished the combing and powdering, and have checked that your cat's eyes and ears are clean, you have finished the grooming routine needed by a pet Persian.

Bathing Your Persian

You should get your Persian cat used to having a bath from an early age. Bath your kitten every now and again even if there is no apparent need; the first bath will be a lot easier if you are dealing with a kitten rather than with a fully grown cat. Most cats will object to being bathed, but if you persist with regular bathing they will get used to the idea, and let you get on with it.

You should find it quite easy to bath a small kitten single-handed in a sink or basin, and rinse it under the taps. But you may need help with an adult cat. If it is at all possible, I recommend that two people tackle the task, one to hold, shampoo, and talk to the cat, while the other rinses it with the shower. This operation is usually best attempted in a bath tub.

Before you embark on bathing your Persian, make sure that you have a suitable shampoo. Never use a shampoo intended for adult humans, nor one intended for dogs, as anti-flea insecticides contained in some dog shampoos can poison cats. Pet shops stock plenty of shampoos designed specifically for cats. Alternatively, you could use a baby shampoo. You will also need one or two large towels with which to rub your cat dry.

Place the cat in the bath, talking gently as you do so. Using lukewarm water, thoroughly wet the cat, making sure that the water reaches all the way through the fur to the cat's skin. Wet the cat's face, taking great care to keep water and shampoo out of its eyes and ears. You will probably not need to use shampoo on your cat's face; water alone should be enough to clean such a sensitive area. When the cat is thoroughly wet, gently rub in the shampoo, paying particular attention to the area underneath the tail, as this often gets soiled.

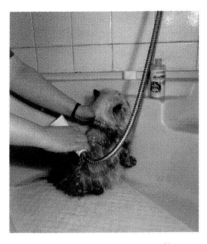

Place your Persian on a non-slip mat in the bath, then proceed to wet the coat through using the shower attachment.

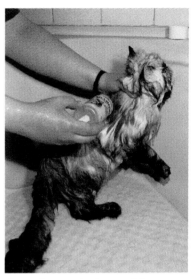

Once the coat is thoroughly soaked, apply the shampoo.

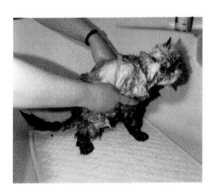

Gently rub the shampoo all over the cat's coat, taking care to avoid the eyes and ears.

Carefully rinse out all traces of shampoo from the cat's coat.

Photos - Shaun Flannery.

Persian Cats

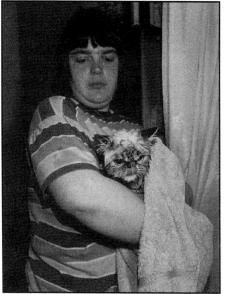

Once rinsed, wrap the cat in a towel and rub gently all over.
Photo - Shaun Flannery.

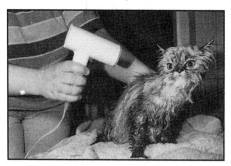

If the cat will let you, finish the drying process with a hair-dryer.
Photo - Shaun Flannery.

Rinse the cat thoroughly, using a hand shower if possible. It is very important that all the shampoo is rinsed out. Do not forget the stomach area and the chest. When all the shampoo has been washed away, gently squeeze the cat's fur to remove any excess water, then wrap the cat in a towel and place it on a table. Gently rub the cat all over with a towel.

There are several different ways of getting the cat completely dry. Your best bet is to use a hair-dryer if your cat will co-operate, but be careful not to hold the dryer too close to the cat's body, as this could burn its skin. Many cats object to hair-dryers and refuse to go near them, so do not frighten your cat by forcing him to accept it; opt for an alternative method. You could try putting the cat in a secure pen (a kitten pen or a travelling box) and then position a fan heater or hair-dryer to blow warm air over the cat. Again, do make sure your cat is not frightened by this, and that the heat does not become too great. If your cat will not stand for this approach either, the only other solution is to put it in a warm room, and let it dry off naturally. A wet cat will naturally seek warmth, so if the room has a fire, so much the better. Never leave a damp cat in a cold room, as this could be very dangerous.

A condition known as "stud tail" can occur in Persian cats from time to time: the glands at the base of the tail start producing an excess of grease which mats the tail fur and makes it greasy to the touch. This condition can present a very annoying problem when Persians are shown. Its name is misleading, as stud tail can affect queens and neuters as well as studs.

If your cat is affected, lift the grease from its tail before bathing it in the normal way. Do this by washing the area thoroughly with washing-up liquid, gently using a toothbrush to rub the tail. Once the cat is dry, avoid unnecessary combing of the tail base, as the condition is aggravated by stimulation of the glands.

The end result: a nice clean Persian!
Photo - Shaun Flannery.

Persian Cats

Show Grooming

Grooming your Persian for a show is a different matter from the simple routine needed by a pet cat. Show grooming is a fine art, the perfection of which require a lot of practice. There are probably nearly as many approaches to grooming Persians for showing as there are Persian breeders, and almost everyone will have his own special method. What I have described below is the approach taught to me when I started showing.

It is not enough to start grooming your cat a week or so before the event: a show Persian must always be well-groomed. Teasing out knots or matted fur may very well ruin the coat. A Persian cat needs intensive preparation for about a week before the show. Since most cat shows are held on Saturdays, the following timetable assumes that this is the case with your show.

It is very important to groom every inch of your Persian's body. Knots will easily form on the tummy and in the armpits.
Photo - Shaun Flannery.

- On the Saturday before the show you should groom the cat thoroughly and powder its coat. First powder the cat all over its body, avoiding its face. Gently rub in the powder all the way down to the roots of the fur, then comb the coat through using the moulting comb with teeth of varying lengths. Carefully comb through all the fur on the stomach, making very sure there are no knots. Comb the cat's trousers, while it is still on your lap, ensuring they are knot-free. Then stand the cat on a table and comb the tail from the tip towards the body. The fur should part in the middle of the tail, and should then be brushed outwards. If the tail is well furnished, the finished effect should leave the tail as wide as cat's body. Now comb the trousers on the hind legs a second time, then comb through all the fur on the cat's back. Once you have finished this, comb the fur forward, over the cat's head, and comb the cat's ruff upwards, so that it makes a frame around its face. Finally, comb the cheek fur forward as well and, as a finishing touch, use a brush to coax the fur even further forward, gently fluffing up the cat's coat. You will have succeeded if, rather than falling straight down at its side, your cat's coat stands right out all over its body. You should repeat this procedure once a day until Tuesday or Wednesday, when the cat must be bathed.

- Because shampoo will remove some of the natural lustre of a Persian's coat, bathing should take place no later than the Wednesday, giving the coat ample time to recover. Wait until the cat is completely dry before continuing your preparation. Be patient: you should never comb a wet cat! The experience would be very unpleasant for the animal, and would pull out and lose a lot of fur unnecessarily. Once the cat is dry, you can repeat the show-grooming routine for that day.

- On the day after the bath (Thursday) comb and brush the cat thoroughly, then powder it. On this occasion use more powder than usual, and do not brush it out - leave it in the coat.

- On Friday (the day before the show) do not use any powder. Groom the cat as before, making sure every last trace of powder is removed. A good way of checking whether any powder is left in the cat's coat is to blow into the fur. When you have finished, make sure the cat's ears and eyes are clean, and that its claws have been trimmed.

You are now ready for the show! (More tips follow in chapter 8.)

Finish off each grooming session using a soft-bristled brush.
Photo - TFH.

varieties 7
of the persian
cat

Persian cats come in a great variety of colours, and each variety has a breed number by which the exact colour and breed of a cat can be identified. For example: Black Persian Longhair is the first breed type (number one); breed number two denotes the Blue Eyed White Persian Longhair; and so on. What follows in this chapter is a complete list and description of all Persian type longhairs, as described by the Governing Council of the Cat Fancy (GCCF) in its Standard of Points booklet. The information is reproduced by kind permission of the GCCF.

Please note: I have only listed the GCCF's descriptions of each variety, NOT the full standard (which includes faults, scales of points, etc).

Self Longhair

Black Longhair (1)
Colour - Lustrous dense black, sound and even in colour, free from rustiness, shading, markings or white hairs. Nose leather, eye rims and paw pads black.
Note: Black kittens often show grey or rusting in their coats; this should not be unduly penalised.
Eyes - Copper or deep orange.

White Longhair (2 series)
Colour - Pure white, free of marks or shade of any kind. Nose leather, eye rims and paw pads pink.
Note: White kittens sometimes have a few coloured hairs on the head and should not be penalised for this.
Eyes - See 2, 2a and 2b.

Blue-Eyed White Longhair (2)
Eyes - Decidedly blue, deeper shades preferred.

This blue-eyed White Persian exhibits what is known as an "open" face, a round face with broad cheeks and a short nose, but no exaggerations. Photo - Isabelle Francais.

Orange-Eyed White (2a)
Eyes - Copper or deep orange.

Odd-Eyed White Longhair (2b)
Eyes - One eye blue and one eye orange or deep copper.

Blue Longhair (3)
Colour - Medium to pale blue, sound and even in colour, free from shadings, markings or white hairs. Nose leather, eye rims and paw pads blue-grey.
Eyes - Copper or deep orange.

Red Self Longhair (4)
Colour - Deep rich red, free of white hairs, sound and even in colour, although slight shading on the forehead and legs is acceptable. Nose leather, eye rims and paw pads deep pink.
Eyes - Copper or deep orange.

Cream Longhair (5)
Colour - Pale to medium cream, sound and even in colour without a white undercoat, free from shading, markings or white hairs. Nose leather, eye rims and paw pads pink.
Eyes - Copper or deep orange.

Chocolate Longhair (50b)
Colour - Medium to dark chocolate, warm in tone, sound and even in colour, free from shading, markings or white hairs. Nose leather, eye rims and paw pads chocolate.
Note: Chocolate kittens sometimes show greying in the coat and should not be unduly penalised for this.
Eyes - Copper or deep orange.

This Red Persian shows the typical short, flat face of the show quality Persian.
Photo - Isabelle Francais.

Cream Self Persian.
Photo - Isabelle Francais.

Lilac Longhair (50c)
Colour - Lilac, warm in tone, sound and even in colour, free from shading, markings or white hairs. Nose leather, eye rims and paw pads lilac.
Eyes - Copper or deep orange.

Smoke Longhair

A Smoke is a cat of contrasts, the undercoat being as white as possible, with the tips shading to the appropriate colour or colours relevant to the breed number. The darker points should be most defined on the back, head and feet, and the light points on frill, flanks and ear tufts. All Smokes have orange or copper eyes.

Black Smoke Longhair (6)
Body - Black shading to silver on the sides and flanks. Mask and feet black with no markings. Frill and ear tufts silver. Undercoat as nearly white as possible.

Blue Smoke Longhair (6a)
The above is also the standard for the Blue Smoke, reading "Blue" where "Black" appears.

Chocolate Smoke Longhair (6b) (Preliminary standard)
Body - Chocolate shading to silver on the sides and flanks. Mask and feet chocolate with no markings. Frill and ear tufts silver. Undercoat as nearly white as possible.

Lilac Smoke Longhair (6c) (Preliminary)
The above is also the standard for the Lilac Smoke, reading "Lilac" where "Chocolate" appears.

Red Smoke Longhair (6d)
Body - Red shading to white on the sides and flanks. Mask and feet red with no markings. Frill and ear tufts white. Undercoat as nearly white as possible. Tabby markings not permitted.

Tortie Smoke Longhair (6e)
Tipping to comprise black, red and cream, well broken into patches.

Cream Smoke Longhair (6f)
Body - Cream shading to white on the sides and flanks. Mask and feet cream with no markings. Frill and ear tufts white. Undercoat as nearly white as possible. Tabby markings not permitted.

Blue-Cream Smoke Longhair (6g)
Tipping to consist of blue and cream softly intermingled. Tipping of any intensity acceptable. Nose leather blue, pink or combination of the two.

Chocolate Tortie Smoke Longhair (6h) (Preliminary)

Body - Chocolate and shades of red, well broken into patches, shading to silver on the sides and flanks. Mask and feet densely pigmented and showing patches of chocolate and shades of red. Frill and ear tufts silver. Undercoat as nearly white as possible. Nose leather and paw pads chocolate and/or pink.

Lilac Tortie Smoke Longhair (6j) (Preliminary)

Body - Lilac and cream finely intermingled, shading to silver on the sides and flanks. Mask and feet densely pigmented and finely intermingled lilac and cream. Frill and ear tufts silver. Undercoat as nearly white as possible. Nose leather and paw pads lilac and/or cream.

Chinchilla (10)

Colour - Undercoat pure white. Coat on the back, flanks, head, ears and tail tipped with black; this tipping to be evenly distributed, thus giving the characteristic sparkling silver appearance. The legs may be very slightly shaded with the tipping, but the chin, ear furnishings, stomach and chest must be pure white; any tabby markings or brown or cream tinges are defects. Nose leather brick-red, and the visible skin on eyelids and paw pads black or dark brown. Eyes - Emerald or blue-green.

Adult Chinchilla Persian of the British type.
Photo - Jeff Spall.

Cameo Longhair

A Cameo is a cat of contrasts. The undercoat should be as white as possible, with the tips shading to red or tortoiseshell in the red series (51) and to cream or blue-cream in the cream series (52). The deepest intensity of colour should be most defined on the mask, along the spine from head to tip of tail, and on legs and feet; the light points should occur on the frill, flanks, under-surfaces and ear furnishings. The eyes should be deep orange or copper.

Red Shell Cameo (51 1)
Characteristic sparkling silver appearance, lightly dusted with rose pink. Nose leather and pads pink

Red Shaded Cameo (51 2)
White evenly shaded with red giving the overall effect of a red mantle. Nose leather and pads pink.Tabby markings undesirable.

Tortie Cameo (51 4)
To comprise black, red, and cream, broken into patches. Colours to be rich and bright and well broken into patches on the face. Tipping of any intensity acceptable. Solid colour on legs or feet undesirable. Nose leather black, pink or a combination of the two.

Cream Shell Cameo (52 1)
Characteristic sparkling silver appearance, lightly dusted with cream. Nose leather and pads pink.

Cream Shaded Cameo (52 2)
White evenly shaded with cream, giving overall effect of a cream mantle. Nose leather and pads pink. Tabby markings undesirable.

Blue-Cream Cameo (52 4)
Tipping to consist of blue and cream, softly intermingled. Tipping of any intensity acceptable. Nose leather blue, pink or combination of the two.

Pewter (53)
Colour - White evenly shaded with black giving an overall effect of a pewter mantle. White undercoat; legs shaded; chin, ear furnishings and stomach white. Nose leather brick red outlined with black; visible skin on eyelids and on pads on feet to be black or dark brown.
Eyes - Orange or copper.

Golden Persian (54)
Colour - Undercoat apricot deepening to gold. Chin, ear furnishings, stomach and chest pale apricot; nose leather brick red; rims of eyes, lips and nose outlined with seal brown or black. Back, flanks, head and tail any shade of gold sufficiently tipped with seal brown or black to give a golden appearance; the general tipping effect to be much darker than that of the usual Chinchilla. Tipping on tail will be heavier than on the body. Legs may be shaded; back of legs from paw to heel solid colour of seal brown or black. Paw pads seal brown or black. Golden kittens often show Tabby markings and may be of unsound colour.
Eyes - Green or blue-green.

Shaded Silver Persian.
The Shaded Silver is basically a
darker version of the Chinchilla.
Photo - Isabelle Francais.

Shaded Silver queen with kitten.
Photo - TFH.

Shaded Silver Longhair (55)
(Preliminary)
Colour - Undercoat pure white with a black tipping shading down from the back to the flanks and lighter on the face and the legs. Face and above side of the tail must be tipped. Chin, chest, stomach, inside of the legs and underside of the tail must be pure white. The general effect to be much darker than the Chinchilla. The tipping can be one-third of the complete hair length and must be as even as possible. Hair on the foot pad to the joint may be shaded to black. Legs to be the same tone as the face. Nose leather must be brick red. Rims of eyes, lips and nose must be outlined with black. Paw pads black or Seal. No barring on the legs is permissible. Any tabby markings or brown or cream tinges are defects.
Eyes - Emerald green or blue-green, emerald green preferred.

Tabby Longhair

Coat pattern - markings on Longhaired Tabbies should be clearly defined and dense in colour with no brindling. On the forehead a letter "M" should be visible. There should be an unbroken line shaped like a butterfly running back from the corner of the eye, with pencillings on the cheek, and lines running over the back of the head extending to the shoulder markings. On the neck and chest there should be unbroken necklaces, the more the better. There should also be a line running down the spine from the butterfly to the tail, with a clear line running parallel on each side. These three stripes down the back should be separated from each other by stripes of the ground colour. Each flank should have an oyster marking. The markings on each side should be identical. The abdominal area should be spotted. Legs should be identical, each barred with bracelets from the body markings to the feet. The tail should be well ringed.

Allowances will be made for diffusion of Classic Tabby markings in cats showing extra-long or full-flowing coats.

Silver Tabby Longhair (7)
Clear silver ground colour. Markings dense black. Silver frill. Eyes green or hazel. Nose leather brick red with black outline. Pads black.

Brown Tabby Longhair (8)
Rich tawny sable ground colour with dense black markings. Eyes orange or copper (no green rim). Nose leather brick red. Pads black or

Photo - Isabelle Francais.

**Blue Tabby Longhair (8a)
(Preliminary)**
Pale blue ground colour with a fawn cast giving distinctive "blue biscuit" base colour. Markings to be a darker even blue, solid to the roots and providing good contrast. Lips and chin should show no differentiation from ground colour. Nose leather pink or blue. Pads dark blue.
Eyes - Brilliant copper or orange.

**Chocolate Tabby Longhair (8b)
(Preliminary)**
Colour - Rich cho
markings on a bronze
Nose leather choco
rimmed with choco
and paw pads chocolِ
Eyes - Hazel or coppe

**Lilac Tabby Longhair (8c)
(Preliminary)**
Lilac markings on a beige agouti ground. Nose leather faded lilac or pink rimmed with faded lilac. Eye rims and paw pads faded lilac.
Eyes - Hazel or copper.

Red Tabby Longhair (9)
Rich red ground colour with markings of deeper richer red. Eyes orange or copper (no green rim). Nose leather deep pink. Pads deep pink.

**Twelve-week
Tabby Persiaı**
Photo - Jeff Spaıı.

Tortie Tabby Longhair (Preliminary Standard)

A Tortie Tabby is a Tabby cat in which the tabby pattern is overlaid with shades of red or cream. Both elements, Tabby and Tortie, must be clearly visible. Coat pattern as for Tabby Longhairs. The eyes should be orange or copper.

Tortie Tabby Longhair (8e) (Preliminary)

The base tabby pattern should consist of dense black markings on a brilliant coppery brown agouti background which has been overlaid with shades of red. Nose leather brick red and/or pink. Paw pads black and/or pink depending on the distribution of the red.

Chocolate Tortie Tabby Longhair (8h) (Preliminary)

The base tabby pattern should consist of rich chocolate markings on a bronze agouti background overlaid with shades of red. Nose leather chocolate and/or pink. Paw pads chocolate and/or pink depending on the distribution of the red.

Blue Tortie Tabby Longhair (8g) (Preliminary)

The base tabby pattern should consist of deep blue markings on a cool toned beige agouti background overlaid with shades of cream. Nose leather blue and/or pink. Paw pads blue and/or pink depending on the distribution of the cream.

Lilac Tortie Tabby Longhair (8j) (Preliminary)

The base tabby pattern should consist of lilac markings on a beige agouti background which has been overlaid with shades of cream. Nose leather faded lilac and/or pink. Paw pads faded lilac and/or pink depending on the distribution of the cream.

Tortoiseshell, Tortie and White, Bi-colour and Van-Pattern Longhair

The eyes should be deep orange or copper.

The Van-Pattern Persian has markings like those of the Turkish Van.
Photo - Isabelle Francais.

Blue-Cream Longhair (13)
Blue and cream, pastel in tone and softly intermingled throughout the coat to the extremities.

Chocolate Tortie Longhair (11b) (Provisional standard)
Chocolate well broken by shades of red throughout the coat to the extremities.
Note: Some kittens may show greying in the chocolate fur. This is not a fault and an otherwise good exhibit should not be unduly penalised for it.

Lilac-Cream Longhair (11c) (Provisional)
Lilac and cream, pastel in tone and softly intermingled throughout the coat to the extremities.

Tortoiseshell Longhair (11)
Black well broken by shades of red throughout the coat to the extremities.
Note: Some kittens may show greying in the black fur. This is not a fault and an otherwise good exhibit should not be unduly penalised for it.

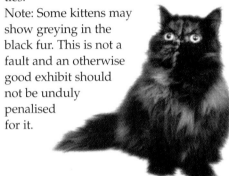

Tortoiseshell. This variety is sex linked and occurs in females only.
Photo - Vincent Serbin.

Seven week old Blue-Cream Persian kitten Photo - Jeff Spall.

Tortoiseshell and White Longhair

Base colour to be broken into patches, the patches of colour to be distinct and without scattered white hairs. Not less than one-third and not more than half the coat to be white; the face to show both colour and white; the limbs white with some colour allowed. Some white on the tail is acceptable.

Tortoiseshell and White.
Photo - Isabelle Francais.

Tortie and White Longhair (12 1)
Base colour black and shades of red.

Blue Tortie and White Longhair (12 2)
Base colour medium to pale blue and cream.

Chocolate Tortie and White Longhair (12 3) (Preliminary)
Base colour chocolate and shades of red.

Lilac Tortie and White Longhair (12 4) (Preliminary)
Base colour lilac and cream.

Tortie Tabby and White Longhair

Tortie Tabbies must show both elements: tabby and tortoiseshell.

Tortie Tabby and White Longhair (12a6t) (Preliminary)

Base colour Brown Tabby which has been patched and overlaid with shades of red.

Blue Tortie Tabby and White Longhair (12a8t) (Preliminary)

Base colour Blue Tabby which has been patched and overlaid with shades of cream.

Chocolate Tortie Tabby and White Longhair (12a9t) (Preliminary)

Base colour Chocolate Tabby which has been patched and overlaid with shades of red.

Lilac Tortie Tabby and White Longhair (12a10t) (Preliminary)

Base colour Lilac Tabby which has been patched and overlaid with shades of cream.

Bi-Colour Longhair

Any solid colour or tabby (except silver) and white; the patches of colour to be distinct and without scattered white hairs. Not less than one-third and not more than half the coat to be white; the face to show both colour and white; the limbs white with some colour allowed. Some white on the tail is acceptable.

The underside of a Bi-colour is essentially white.
Photo - Isabelle Francais.

Bi-Colours, Solid Colours and White

Coloured fur to be sound and even in colour, and free from any tabby markings; the white fur to be pure white and free from marks or shading of any kind.

Black and White Bi-colour Longhair (12a1)
Lustrous dense black, free from rustiness, shading, markings or white hairs.

Blue and White Bi-colour Longhair (12a2)
Medium to pale blue, free from shading, markings or white hairs.

Chocolate and White Bi-colour Longhair (12a3)
Chocolate, warm in tone, free from shading, markings or white hairs.

Black and white Bi-colour.
Photo - Isabelle Francais.

Lilac and White Bi-colour Longhair (12a4)
Lilac, warm in tone, free from shading, markings or white hairs.

Red and White Bi-colour Longhair (12a5)
Deep rich red, free from white hairs; slight shading in any red on the forehead and legs acceptable.

Red and white Bi-colour.
Photo - Isabelle Francais.

Cream and White Bi-colour Longhair (12a7)
Pale to medium cream without a white undercoat, free from shading, markings or white hairs.

Bi-Colour, Tabby Colours and White

Coloured fur to show the tabby pattern on the appropriate ground colour; the white fur to be pure white and free from marks or shading of any kind.

Brown Tabby and White Longhair (12a1t) (Preliminary)
Black markings on a rich sable agouti background.

Blue Tabby and White Longhair (12a2t) (Preliminary)
Blue markings on a beige agouti background.

Chocolate Tabby and White Longhair (12a3t) (Preliminary)
Chocolate markings on a bronze agouti background.

Lilac Tabby and White Longhair (12a4t) (Preliminary)
Lilac markings on a pale beige agouti background.

Red Tabby and White Longhair (12a5t) (Preliminary)
Rich red markings on an apricot agouti background.

Cream Tabby and White Longhair (12a7t) (Preliminary)
Cream markings on a paler cream agouti background.

Van Distribution Bi-Colour and Tri-Colour

Coats should be basically white with colour confined to the head, ears and tail. For perfection there should be no colour on the body or legs, but up to three small "spots" of colour may be allowed in an otherwise excellent example of the breed. The coloured areas need not be of a required or uniform shape, and whilst the markings should preferably show a visual balance, symmetry is not essential. Tails should be fully coloured.

Bi-Colours

Black and White Van Longhair (12a1w) (Preliminary)
Lustrous dense black, free from rustiness, shading, markings or white hairs.

Lilac and White Van Longhair (12a4w) (Preliminary)
Lilac, warm in tone, free from shading, markings or white hairs.

Blue and White Van Longhair (12a2w) (Preliminary)
Medium to pale blue, free from shading, markings or white hairs.

Red and White Van Longhair (12a5w) (Preliminary)
Deep rich red, free from white hairs, slight shading of any red on the forehead is acceptable.

Chocolate and White Van Longhair (12a3w) (Preliminary)
Chocolate, warm in tone, free from shading, markings or white hairs.

Cream and White Van Longhair (12a7w) (Preliminary)
Pale to medium cream without a white undercoat, free from shading, markings or white hairs.

Tri-Colours

Tortie and White Van Longhair (12 1w) (Preliminary)
Tortie base colour to be black and shades of red.

Chocolate Tortie and White Van Longhair (12 3w) (Preliminary)
Tortie base colour to be chocolate and shades of red.

Blue Tortie and WhiteVan Longhair (12 2w) (Preliminary)
Tortie base colour to be medium pale blue and cream.

Lilac Tortie and White Van Longhair (12 3w) (Preliminary)
Tortie base colour to be lilac and cream.

Colourpoint

The points (mask, ears, legs and feet, and tail) should be as evenly coloured as possible. There should be a good contrast between the points and body colour. Light body shading, if present, to be confined to the shoulders and flanks, and should tone with the points. The mask should cover the entire face, including the chin and whisker pads; it should not extend over the head, although the mask of a mature male is more extensive than that of a mature female. The points should be free of white hairs and any areas of non-pigmented fur. Eyes should be brilliant and pure in colour, decidedly blue.
Note:The rate at which point colour develops is variable; the dilute colours take the longest.

Persian Cats

Solid Point Colours

The colour on all the points should be evenly matched in tone and free from any sign of patchiness. Nose leather, eye rims and paw pads to tone with the point colour.

Seal Point (13b1)
Points seal brown with toning creamy white body colour.

Blue Point (13b2)
Points blue with glacial white body colour.

Chocolate Point (13b3)
Points chocolate in colour and warm in tone, with ivory white body colour.

Lilac Point (13b4)
Points lilac in colour and warm in tone, with magnolia white body colour.

Red Point (13b5)
Points rich red with apricot white body colour.

Cream Point (13b7)
Points cream with toning creamy-white body colour.

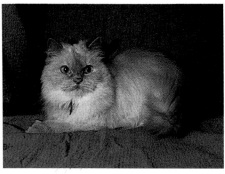

Blondie, the author's first Persian, a Cream Colourpoint. Although not of show quality, she is very beautiful.
Photo - Shaun Flannery.

Blue Point Colourpoint Persian. The Colourpoint is known as the Himalayan in America.
Photo - Isabelle Francais.

Tortie Point Colours

The colour on the points should be the base seal blue, chocolate or lilac, which has been broken with shades of red or cream. Ideally, all the points should show some red or cream. A blaze is permissible. Nose, leather, eye rims and paw pads to tone with the point colour.

Seal Tortie Point (13b6)
Points seal, broken with shades of red; toning creamy body colour.

Blue-Cream Point (13b8)
Points blue and shades of cream; glacial to creamy white body colour.

The Colourpoint Persian comes in as many as 20 different points varieties. Here is a Seal Tortie Point. Photo - Isabelle Francais.

Chocolate Tortie Point (13b9)
Points chocolate and shades of red with ivory to apricot white body colour.

Lilac-Cream Point (13b10)
Points lilac and shades of cream with magnolia to creamy white body colour.

Seal Point Colourpoint (see Page 72) in the form of the author's prize-winning queen, Cheval Cressida.
Photo - Shaun Flannery.

Tabby Point Colours

There should be a clearly defined "M" marking the forehead, "spectacles" markings round the eyes and spotted whisker pads. The front legs have broken rings from the toes upwards; barring on the hind legs is confined to the front of the upper leg and thigh, the back of the leg from toe to hock should be solid point colour. Ears solid but showing clear "thumb marks" which are less apparent in dilute colours and mottled in the Tortie Tabby Points. Hair inside the ears is lighter, giving the appearance of a pale rim; ear tufts are lighter in colour. Tails have broken rings. Nose leather pinkish outlined with pigment, or to tone with the points. Eye rims and paw pads to tone with the points.

Non-Tortie Tabby Point Colours

These colours show distinct tabby markings, although they are much more subtle in their dilute colours.

Seal Tabby Point (13b11)
Seal brown markings on a pale brown agouti background; body colour a toning creamy white. Nose fur may be ginger towards the leather.

Blue Tabby Point (13b12)
Blue markings on a light beige agouti background; body colour glacial white. Nose fur may be fawn towards the leather.

Chocolate Tabby Point (13b13)
Chocolate markings on a light bronze agouti background; body colour ivory white. Nose fur may be bronze towards the leather.

Lilac Tabby Point (13b14)
Lilac markings on a pale beige agouti background; body colour magnolia white.

Red Tabby Point (13b15)
Rich red markings on a light apricot agouti background; body colour apricot white.

Cream Tabby Point (13b17)
Cream markings on a paler cream agouti background; body colour a toning creamy white.

Tortie Tabby Point Colours

These colours show the normal tabby pattern which has been patched and overlaid with shades of red or cream. The extent and distribution of the tortie areas is not important providing that both elements, Tortie and Tabby, are clearly visible.

Seal Tortie Tabby Point (13b16)
Seal brown markings on a pale brown agouti background overlaid and patched with shades of red; toning creamy body colour.

Chocolate Tortie Tabby Point (13b19)
Chocolate markings on a light bronze agouti background, overlaid and patched in shades of red; body colour ivory to apricot white.

Blue-Cream Tabby Point (13b18)
Blue markings on a light beige agouti background, overlaid and patched with shades of cream; body colour glacial to creamy white.

Lilac-Cream Tabby Point (13b20)
Lilac markings on a pale beige agouti background, overlaid with shades of cream; body colour magnolia to creamy white.

Blue-Cream Persian (see Page 65). This colour is obtained by mixing the Blue with the Cream. It is a diluted version of the Tortoiseshell and is sometimes known as Dilute Tortie or Blue Tortie.
Photo - Isabelle Francais.

showing your persian **8**

Why Show ?

Showing your cat or cats can be a lot of fun. You will meet many people with a common interest, and it is a real thrill to compete for prizes with your cat, perhaps even making it to Champion.

If you intend to breed, it is almost imperative that you show your cat. In this way you will learn what an ideal Persian should look like, and have a chance to find a potential stud for your queen. It is not advisable to breed from a queen who is not of show quality. There are a lot of pet quality kittens in the world already (mainly non-pedigree), and it is these which are most likely to end up unwanted. You are far more likely to be able to find a good home for show quality kittens than for kittens bred from non-show parents. Showing a cat will help you acquire a fairly good idea of whether or not it is a cat worth breeding from - and prospective buyers will often want to know how well your kittens' parents have done at shows.

The Show Quality Persian

As discussed earlier, not all purebred Persians are necessarily of show quality. In almost every litter there will be a kitten which falls below show standard, so if you want to buy a cat for showing purposes, you must make your requirement very clear to the breeder. The quality of Persian cats at shows is usually very high, so it is simply a waste of time and money entering a mediocre cat. Before embarking on your new kitten's show career, make sure you transfer its registration into your own name. This is vital if you want to exhibit your cat.

What does a show quality Persian look like? Well, it must be healthy, but of course that is not all. The GCCF standard of points lists a type standard for each group of Persian cat - the Selfs, the Colourpoints and so on. This standard may vary very slightly within the different groups, but in general it is the same throughout. All Persian cats should have the same shape of body, face, ears etc.

The head should be round and large, with a slightly rounded top and great spacing between the ears; the cheeks should be full. The nose should be short, or "flat", with a "break" above; in the "classic" or "open" type Persian (which is the ideal) the break is found between the cat's eyes, with the nose slightly below the line of the eyes. In the

A far cry from your average moggy. Champion Rejuta Dolly Daydream, a Brown Tabby Persian with owner Val Sargison. Photo - Nick Mays.

"ultra" type Persian, the nose is on the same level as the eyes, giving a very flat profile. This is not allowed in most varieties of Persians, however: it is considered a fault in the standard of points.

The eyes are large and round. They should be set well apart, and must be of the appropriate colour for that particular variety.

The ears should be small with rounded tips.

The teeth are important - the cat's mouth will be checked at every show. A Persian cat should have an even bite, and must be neither undershot (which is quite common) nor overshot (which is rare).

The body should be cobby, with short, thick legs. The cat should be big and well muscled.

The tail should be short, and must be free from any defects, including kinks. Any cat with a tail defect will be very heavily penalised at a show, and should not be used for breeding, because tail defects are usually hereditary. The fur on a Persian's tail should be long and dense. When it is brushed out the tail should be almost as wide as the body.

The coat should be long, thick, and of good texture. It is very important that the cat is groomed to perfection; judges will pay a great deal of attention to its presentation.

The colour should conform to the standard set for its particular variety (see chapter 7).

Persian Cats

When to Show

Cat shows are held throughout the year, in most parts of the country. You can find out about forthcoming shows in advance by looking out for advertisements in the weekly magazine *Cats*. Published monthly, *Cat World* also carries some show advertising. In addition, a complete list of shows being held over a 12-month period (June-May) is available from the GCCF.

Cats are not eligible for showing until they are at least 14 weeks old and so, if your kitten was born on 5 January, you are not permitted to show it until 13 April: not even one or two days beforehand. Pregnant and lactating queens with kittens younger than three months old are also ineligible and may not be shown.

You will obviously want your cat to be in the best possible condition when you show it. For many Persians, this will mean the summer is not a good showing season. Because longhaired cats often shed some of their coat to keep them cool when it is hot, they will usually look better in colder weather. It is not impossible to show a Persian cat during the summer, however. All cats are individuals, and yours may be in full coat even then.

Different Types of Shows

The cat shows held in Britain fall into several different categories. Most common is the Championship Show, a large event offering classes for almost every breed and colour. Shows of this type will award Challenge Certificates to winning adult cats. A cat gaining three such certificates (awarded by three different judges) will be made up to a Champion (or, if your cat has been neutered, a Premier). While some Championship shows are open to all breeds of cat, this is not always the case; some are restricted to entrants from one breed group only (Longhairs for example) and some are open only to a single breed of cat (Colourpoint Persians for example).

The Sanction Show is quite rare. It is almost a rehearsal for a championship show: all the arrangements are the same, but no certificates are awarded.

Exemption Shows are smaller events, exempt from some GCCF rules. They usually take place in the summer, and are often held in conjunction with agricultural shows. Challenge Certificates are not awarded; fewer classes are offered than at a Championship show and the entry fee is lower. There may be just one class for all adult Colourpoints, including males and females of any colour - a Championship show would divide the same cats into ten different classes, five different colour classes for each sex.

At the top of the tree is the Supreme Show. This takes the form of a very special show organised annually by the GCCF. The Supreme show is restricted to previous Championship show winners, and your cat must qualify before-hand, usually by winning one or more Challenge certificates. The Supreme show is well worth a visit even if your cat is not among the entrants, as most of Britain's top show cats gather under one roof for the event. The adult winner of the Supreme show is awarded the title Supreme Grand Champion, the neuter winner becomes the Supreme Grand Premier.

Entering the Show

Once you have found a show in which you are interested, the next thing to do is to send for the show schedule. Write to the show manager including a stamped addressed envelope, and he should return a copy within a few days. Beware of leaving it to the last minute. It is wiser to apply for your schedule as soon as it is available, typically about three months before the show. The final date for entries is usually six weeks before the date of the show, and it is important to get your cat entered in good time. Many cat clubs limit the number of entries according to the space available for the show and, as accep-tance is on a first-come, first-served basis, popular shows are likely to close earlier than the published date to avoid over-subscription.

Having received your schedule, you should look through the list of classes and decide which to enter. At most shows, cats are required to enter a minimum of four classes: one "open" class and three other "side" classes; and the entrance fee is likely to cover all four entries. If you wish your cat to be entered in more than four classes, there will be an extra charge. Some shows have a limit on the number of classes any one cat may enter.

First you should look for your Persian cat's appropriate open class: you will find this listed in the Longhair section. An open class is a breed class, where cats compete with others of the same breed; usually also of the same colour and sex. Make sure you choose the right class; there should only be one open class for which your cat is eligible. If you are entering a kitten of less than nine months, you should choose the designated "kitten" open class appropriate to its breed. If your cat is more than nine months old and un-neutered, it should be entered into the appropriate "adult" open class; if your adult cat has been neutered, it should be entered for the appropriate "neuter" open class. If your cat is already a Champion or a Premier, it can also be entered into the appropriate Grand Champion or Grand Premier class, and you are entitled to choose this class instead of the open class if you so wish.

Having identified the correct open class for your cat, it is time to look at the side classes. These will be listed under Longhaired Miscellaneous: this section will also be split into three sections, one each for kittens, adults, and neuters.

In a side class your cat will probably be competing with cats of various breeds, but they will all be Longhairs. Usually the sexes are split into separate classes, but sometimes male and female will compete alongside each other. Side classes often have a large number of entrants: 20 or more is not uncommon. Side classes include "Debutante" (for cats who are entering their first show); "Novice" (for entrants who have never won a first prize); "Limit" (cats who have won no more than four first prizes); "Aristocrat" (cats who have won at least one Challenge or Premier certificate, but are not yet Champions or Premiers); "Breeders" (cats being exhibited by their breeders) and "Non-Breeders" (cats not bred by current owner); "Radius" (for cats whose owners live within a defined locality); and many more.

The choice can be bewildering, so make it a rule always to opt for the lowest possible class for your cat. If it is not already a show prizewinner, enter those classes offered for non-winners. Entering a beginner straight into a limit class could so easily be a waste of money - unless, of course, your cat is exceptional, and you are unlikely to be sure of that until it has entered at least one show!

Having decided upon the best classes for your cat, it is time to fill in the entry form. Take great care in doing this, as errors may result in disqualification. The form will ask for your cat's full official name: make sure you have written it exactly as it appears on the registration certificate, as pet names will not be accepted. You will also need to supply your cat's breed number, which also appears on the registration certificate; its sex (denote male neuter with MN, female neuter with FM, use M for male, and F for female); the cat's exact date of birth; the full names of the cat's sire and dam; the name of your cat's

During judging at GCCF shows, no-one except the judges and their stewards are allowed inside the show hall. The judges move from pen to pen with a trolley to examine each exhibit. Photo - Nick Mays.

breeder; its GCCF registration number; and, of course, the number of each class into which you wish to enter your cat. Finally, do not forget to fill in your own name and address, and sign the declaration by which you agree to abide by the GCCF's show rules (extracts of which are printed on the entry form) and declare that your cats are healthy. You must also calculate how much your entry will cost.

Be sure to take a photocopy of the completed entry form. This will be important should your entry get lost in the post, and it can be useful to have an exact record of the information supplied. If the show catalogue contains erroneous details concerning your cat (a name spelled incorrectly, for example) it may be necessary to prove that you supplied the correct information: in these cases a copy of the form you submitted will be invaluable.

Do not forget to include a cheque or postal order to cover your entry fee. The schedule or the entry form should clearly indicate to whom the cheque should be made payable (usually the club organising the show). Entries will never be accepted unless accompanied by the appropriate fee.

Read the schedule carefully. Some clubs ask for a stamped addressed envelope which they will use to send you a tally and vetting-in pass for your cat, whilst other clubs supply these upon your arrival at the show. Either way, it is always advisable to enclose a stamped addressed envelope or postcard so that the organiser can acknowledge your entry.

Finally, make sure you address your entry to the right person. Large Championship shows often employ several people, each dealing with one or more of the different sections: Longhairs, Siamese/Oriental and so on. A name and telephone number for the manager of the Longhair section will be given in the schedule; contact him (or her) if you have any queries.

Preparing for the Show

A Persian's coat will need careful preparation before a show. This has already been described, in the chapter on grooming. It is also a good idea to get your cat used to being handled, including having its teeth inspected. The cat will have to go into a pen during the show. Most cats will accept this quite happily, but again, prior training can pay off. I get my kittens used to being confined by regularly putting them in a large pen overnight. I have also found it helpful to start showing my kittens as early as possible, provided they are in good condition and of a good size. A cat who gets used to shows as a young kitten is more likely to cooperate than a cat taken to its first show as an adult. Although I have not come across many cats who object to being shown, some do not like the palaver. If your cat becomes genuinely distressed at a show, give up and let him stay at home. Not only is it unfair to the animal, but a worried cat is also much more likely to scratch or bite stewards and judges, bringing disqualification.

Show Equipment

All cat shows insist that judges must not be able to identify the owner of any individual cat. No distinguishing features of any kind (including favourite toys) are permitted, and each pen must appear identical. Accordingly you will need certain pieces of show equipment with which to furnish your cat's show pen:

- A white litter tray and cat litter.

- A plain white blanket (special "show blankets" will usually be on sale at the shows). Alternatively a "vet bed" with white or green backing may be used. Distinctive blankets with markings or special edgings are not allowed, nor are cellular blankets.

- Two white bowls: one for water, one for food.

- Narrow white ribbon, used to hang the cat's tally round its neck.

- Cat food. Dry food is probably best because it is less likely to soil the fur of a longhaired cat than tinned food, but remember that you are not allowed to feed your cat until all the open classes have been judged.

- An up-to-date vaccination certificate for your cat.

- A secure travelling box for transporting the cat to the show. Cardboard boxes are not accepted.

In addition to these essentials, there are several other items which may be useful at the show: combs and brushes, eye wipes, tissues, and the show schedule including the photocopy of your entry form. However, if you do find you have left a vital piece of equipment at home, you are almost certain to be able to buy a replacement from one of the trade stands on the show site.

The "Thirteen-Day" Rule

Show cat owners must abide by a GCCF ruling, known as the "13-day" rule, which states that no cat (or any cats living in the same household) may be shown more frequently than once every 14 days, leaving a clear 13 days' break between shows. The rule is intended to minimise the risk of spreading infection. Consequently it extends not only to the cat originally shown, but also to other cats living in the same household. Do make sure you take the rule into account when entering any of your cats into show classes. In any case, they will appreciate not being dragged off to a show every weekend!

The Show Day

So finally the day of the show dawns - and it will probably bring an early start. Most events ask you to arrive between 8.00 am and 10.00 am. Do not make the mistake of arriving at the last possible moment. Remember that as you are showing a Persian, you will need time to groom your cat carefully before the judging gets under way, so the earlier you arrive, the better.

To reduce the risk of travel sickness, it is often a good idea not to feed your cat before you leave for the show. It will do no harm to wait until lunchtime. Alternatively you could offer a quick snack once you have arrived. Before putting your cat into the travelling box, remember to do one final check: it is very important that the cat is completely free of fleas and flea dirt and healthy in every respect.

On arrival at the show hall, your first task will be to collect your cat's tally and vetting-in card, if you have not already received them by post. Then it will be time to queue for the vetting-in.

Most of the exhibitors will be feeling nervous about this stage. Even when you are sure your cat is in tip-top condition it is difficult not to worry that the vet will find something amiss! The slightest problem may cause your cat to be rejected, for example the sight of a flea or dirty ears; or it may be something more serious. If your cat has any skin lesions, however small (even a scratch sustained while playing with another cat) do not bring it to the show. Any skin damage is treated as suspicious ringworm: not only would your cat be rejected instantly, but you would also be barred from showing until you had supplied the GCCF with a veterinary certificate pronouncing all your cats free from ringworm. The stringent procedures are designed to safeguard all show cats, but they can prove costly!

During vetting-in, when a specialist team of vets thoroughly checks each cat, you may be asked to produce your vaccination certificate. If there are no problems, the vet will sign your vetting-in card and your cat will be allowed through into the hall.

The next thing to do is to find the pen allocated to your cat, and furnish it with a blanket, litter tray and water bowl. If you decide to feed your cat at this point, make sure you remove the food bowl before the judging starts - you will be allowed to feed your cat again later in the day. You should place both bowls at the rear of the pen.

Some exhibitors prefer to disinfect the pen before putting their cat and its belongings inside. This is acceptable, but no sprays of any kind are allowed in the show hall, so choose a suitable liquid disinfectant.

Once you have prepared the pen, you can take your cat out of its

To remain anonymous, each cat's pen has to be furnished in white only.
Photo - Nick Mays.

travelling box. Now is the time for final grooming, so comb and brush your cat's coat as I have described in the chapter on grooming. Remember not to use any powder; if the eyes have been weeping, wipe below them carefully. When you have finished and your cat looks its best, tie the tally around its neck and place it in its pen.

At about 10.00 am, the judging will start and all exhibitors must leave the show hall. There is usually a nearby cafeteria at which to wait, or perhaps a balcony overlooking the hall where it may be possible to catch a glimpse of the judging. The judges and their stewards will walk around the show hall wheeling a small table on which to examine each cat. The table will be disinfected every time a different cat is examined, and the judges and stewards will disinfect their hands between handling each animal. Exhibitors are not allowed to return to their cats until the judging is more or less complete, usually about 1.00 pm.

Persian Cats

Judging of a Red Persian. The steward holds the cat while the judge examines the cat's tail for defects.
Photo - Nick Mays.

Judging of a Chinchilla Persian.
Photo - Nick Mays.

Upon leaving the hall, you should collect a show catalogue. These are usually made available as the judging begins. Check that all your cat's details are correct. You should report any discrepancies immediately to the Longhair section manager, who (along with all the show's section managers) will be on hand to deal with any problems. The catalogue will also tell you what competition your cat is facing.

Then you must wait. Results are posted on the award board as they become available. Without doubt this is the most exciting part of the day; no experience compares with standing in front of the award board, waiting for the results of your cat's open class to be revealed!

If your cat is a winner, the results sheet will indicate its placing by displaying the appropriate ranking alongside the cat's pen number. So if your cat is in pen 76 and you see "76-2" on the results sheet, your cat has been placed second in the class. If your cat came first, winning a Challenge certificate in the process, the result will be followed by the letters CC or Ch; or PC if a Premier certificate has been won by a neuter.

Judges will also award a Best of Breed to the best cat of a particular colour, so if Blue Persians are divided into two classes according to their sex, the best of the two winners will be awarded Best of Breed. This honour does not signify the best overall cat of a variety - there may be three Best of Breed Blue Persians: an adult, a neuter, and a kitten. Most shows will select a winning cat from each section (the best Longhair, Oriental, British Shorthair etc), and some will go on to choose an overall Best in Show cat from the ranks of section winners.

Well known and respected Persian judge Enid Burrows examines a White Persian. Photo - Nick Mays.

Prizes on offer usually include trophies, cards and rosettes, but some shows award prize money. Certificates are only awarded to winners of open classes; winning one of the side classes will not count towards making up a champion.

In Britain cat judges are very strict. They will sometimes withhold prizes or certificates if they feel no cat in a class is of sufficiently high standard. Even if a cat is the only one entered in a particular class, it will not necessarily win first prize. It may gain only a third placing if it is not deemed worthy of a first.

Even if a first prize is awarded, the judges may withhold the certificate, or decline to award a Best of Breed. Certificates may be withheld either because the cat lacks a breed characteristic, because it needs more grooming, has an undershot bite or perhaps a tail defect, or simply because it is slightly out of condition.

The highest honour any cat can gain, Best in Show at the Supreme Cat Show (UK).
In 1993, this was won by Blue Persian neuter Supreme Grand Premier Firanty Blue Fiori, pictured with proud owner Amanda Bowman.
Photo - Nick Mays.

Do not be disheartened if a judge decides to withhold a prize from your cat: a different judge may disagree (unless there is an obvious fault like a tail kink), and your cat may well improve over time. So do try again!

Once you are allowed to return to the show hall, visit your cat immediately and give him some food. He will probably be very pleased to see you. The show will now be opened to the public, and there will be lots of people admiring your cat. The officials will have moved on to judge the side classes by now. In the meantime prize cards will be displayed on the pens of winning cats, while rosettes will be distributed or made available for collection from the awards table. Show cats will not be allowed to leave the hall until closing time, usually about 5.00 pm.

Once judging has been completed, exhibitors and the general public are let into the hall.
Photo - Nick Mays.

A succesful exhibitor with her Black Smoke Persian.
Photo - Nick Mays.

Making Up Champions and Premiers

One of the most exciting aspects of showing cats is trying to achieve the goal of "making up" a champion. Any adult cat, entire or neuter, is eligible to win certificates, either Challenge Certificates (CCs) if it is entire or Premier Certificates (PCs) if the cat has been neutered. A cat which is awarded three such certificates by three different judges will gain the title Champion or Premier.

Once your cat has become a full champion or premier, it will be eligible to enter Grand Champion or Grand Premier classes in which champions compete against champions, and premiers against premiers. The winner is awarded a Grand Challenge Certificate (GCC) or a Grand Premier Certificate (GPC) - providing, of course, that the judge does not decide to withhold the award. The cat in second place exhibit will receive a Reserve GCC or Reserve GPC. If a cat should gain three "grands" from different judges it will become known as a Grand Champion or Grand Premier. At the Supreme show, it is

possible for a cat to go one step further: if a grand champion or grand premier wins a grand at the Supreme show its grand will count as a "UK Grand". After two such wins, the cat will become known as UK Grand Champion or UK Grand Premier.

But in the final analysis, even if your cat's show career is unremark-able, he or she will still be a very special pet! After all, looks are not everything.

Val Robinson, of the well known Cheval Colourpoints with her Bluepoint queen, Champion Cheval Cherish.
Photo - Nick Mays.

cat clubs 9

If you are interested in showing, you may like to join one or more cat clubs. Membership brings several advantages, such as lower entrance fees for shows organised by your club and the opportunity to enter special classes at club shows. Many clubs also publish very informative membership magazines or journals. Other benefits may include publication of stud or kitten lists.

There are numerous cat clubs in the UK, most of which are affiliated to the GCCF, and therefore governed by GCCF rules. A complete list of affiliated clubs is available from the GCCF. Some clubs may also advertise in *Cats* magazine.

Not all clubs are run along the same lines: some cater for all cats living in a particular area, regardless of breed (eg Yorkshire County Cat Club) while others cater specifically for one breed section (eg North of Britain Longhair Cat Club). Most breed clubs are national (eg Colourpoint Cat Club), and you may find that there is more than one club catering for your breed of cat.

With a few exceptions, most cat clubs require applicants for membership to be proposed by an existing member. A natural choice would be to ask the breeder of your cat to nominate you, as long as he or she is a member of the club you want to join. If you do not know anyone who is already a member, most clubs will accept a vet's signature instead, by way of an assurance that you look after your cats well. For details of how to join a club, you should contact the membership secretary.

View of the Cheval cattery in England, famous for its Colourpoints.
Photo - Shaun Flannery.

breeding 10
persians

Should you breed from your Queen ?

You should think carefully before deciding to breed from a Persian queen; it is not a step to be taken lightly. You may melt at the thought of small fluffy kittens, but caring for a litter can be hard work. Certainly cat breeding should not be undertaken for financial reasons, so do not be tempted into breeding by the prospect of making some money out of it. If you are lucky, you may be left with a small profit from a litter of kittens, but you are more likely to make a loss! The price of a pedigree kitten may sound high, but bear in mind all the expenses that producing such a kitten will involve. Money must be found to pay a fee for blood testing your queen and for the stud fee; feeding her during pregnancy will cost extra; you may face vet's fees if something goes wrong at the birth; rearing the kittens will cost money; and each kitten will incur vaccination and registration costs. A queen is likely to have a small first litter, perhaps three kittens, and if you succumb to the temptation to keep one of her bundles of joy, you will definitely end up out of pocket. If you breed cats it should be because you love your own cat and that particular breed. The ultimate aim is to produce the perfect show cat.

If you keep a female Persian as a pet rather than a show cat, I would strongly recommend you have her neutered. There is no need to let her have a litter first; a queen neutered before producing a litter will not suffer in any way. Indeed in my experience, quite the reverse can be true: a queen who has reared a litter before being neutered is more likely to suffer than if she had been denied the taste of motherhood. My first Colourpoint queen, Blondie, was neutered for medical reasons after rearing one litter and to this day she loves kittens more than anything in life. I am sure she longs in vain for more kittens of her own. So if your queen is simply a pet, do have her neutered.

If you decide you are serious about breeding, make sure your queen is of sufficient quality. I have touched on this in an earlier chapter. Nobody will benefit if you breed from a pet quality queen, and you will find it much easier to find good homes for kittens bred from a show quality female. I must admit that I have made that mistake, breeding from my first queen, Blondie, a pet quality Persian, but I would not do so again. I did ask Blondie's breeder for permission beforehand, and I would not have gone ahead if any objections were raised. I made sure Blondie was mated to a champion stud, a match which at least produced kittens who were better looking than their mother, but it was not until the following generation (Blondie's daughter's offspring) that I was rewarded with show quality kittens.

Having decided your queen is worth breeding from (and remember she must have no defects: the kittens are sure to inherit the likes of a kinked tail), your next step is to make sure she is registered on the GCCF's "active" register. You will not be allowed to register any kittens born from a queen (or stud) which is on the non-active register. If your queen is registered as non-active, her breeder will have had good reason not to want the cat to used for breeding. A cat can only be transferred from the non-active to the active register at the behest of its breeder, and a fee will be payable.

The next question you should address is whether your queen is old enough for motherhood. Many Persian queens mature late in life compared with, say Siamese. She may start "calling" (come into season) at six or eight months, but more often this will not happen until she is between 10 and 14 months of age.

If your queen calls very late it may be possible to mate her at her first call if she is of a good size. If she calls earlier it is usually better to wait, perhaps until her second or third call. Under no circumstances should she be mated before she has reached ten months, and only then if she is large for her age. Most Persian queens will benefit from waiting until the age of about 12 months, but do not wait too long to mate up your queen for the first time: queens allowed to call too often are likely eventually to develop fallopian cysts. It is therefore advisable to have the queen mated before she is two years old. The last, but perhaps most important, consideration is her health. She must be healthy, and in good overall condition, and she should undergo a blood test for Feline Leukaemia Virus (FeLV), carried out by her vet. If the result is negative, you can go ahead with breeding, but the test should be repeated each time you intend to mate your cat, as the result is not reliable for a period longer than three months.

When to breed from your Queen

The timing of your first litter should depend on other considerations besides your queen's age. Before mating up your queen, calculate the time the litter could be expected to arrive. (The average gestation period is 65 days: see **Kittening Chart** at the end of this book.) Make sure your kittens would not be due whilst you are away, on holiday for example, and avoid putting a pregnant queen in a boarding cattery. It will be essential for you to be at home when the kittens are born, which may mean you need to make provision for taking time off from work.

In addition, certain times of year are better than others when it comes to selling the kittens. If you can, talk to other breeders about their experiences. Try to avoid producing kittens which will be ready to leave for new homes at Christmas when they may be bought on impulse as presents, and end up unwanted when the novelty of owning a Persian has worn off. (If your cat does produce kittens due to reach 12 weeks of age during the Christmas period, it may be a good idea to advise inquirers that you will not be letting them go until early January.) Nor is it fair to introduce new kittens into a household full of noise and visitors, as many are at that time of year.

Finding a Stud

It is very important that you find a good stud cat, and one which is suitable for your queen. Ideally you will have found him some time before she is ready to be mated. Assuming you do not own such an animal, finding a suitable stud can be a difficult task, and one which is likely to take more than a couple of days.

There are several ways to find a stud. Owners often advertise in cat club publications, in *Cats* magazine, and in the *Cat World* supplement *Show Cats*. In addition, you may be able to make contact with stud owners at shows, or the breeder of your queen may be able to recommend a stud for her.

There are three different categories of stud: "public", "limited", or "closed". A public stud describes a cat which is available to most queens, as long as they are suitable breeding stock and in good health. A limited stud will often be a top show cat, whose owners will restrict him to mating with good show queens. A cat at closed stud will be unavailable for queens other than those belonging to his owner.

Once you have identified a stud you think may be suitable for your queen, approach his owner to discuss the match. The stud's owner will want to know about your queen in detail: her colour; her show record; her parents and breeder; whether she is a maiden or has previously been mated; and when you wish the mating to take place. If the match is approved, all that remains is to wait for the appropriate time to come around.

The Stud Fee

All stud owners will charge a fee for letting a stud mate your queen as a certain amount of work is involved on their part. It is not simply a question of putting the two cats together for a couple of days and hoping for the best! Close supervision will be required, taking several hours of the stud owner's time, and he will also have to feed and care for your queen during her stay (usually a matter of days).

The amount you pay will vary almost as much as the prices charged for kittens. Some Persian varieties may command slightly lower stud fees than others, while a champion at stud will command a higher price than a stud which has not been made up. Expect to pay somewhere in the region of £60 to £100. It could cost more: when you consider the sum is less than the price paid for a single kitten, it does not seem unreasonable.

The terms and conditions will vary from one stud owner to the next. Most will let you have a free mating if the first one fails, and some will offer you a free mating should the whole litter die, or should the queen produce only one kitten.

Blood Testing

No responsible stud owner will accept a queen for mating unless she has been tested for Feline Leukaemia Virus (FeLV). This particular virus can be passed on by mating, so it is vital that all active cats are tested. Most stud owners will accept a FeLV certificate issued up to three months before the mating date, but some may ask for one less than 24 hours old. Make sure you understand clearly your stud owner's policy well in advance. Some owners may also insist your queen is tested for other diseases, including Feline Infectious Peritonitis (FIP) and Feline Immunodeficiency Virus (FIV).

Check carefully with your vet about testing your queen: not all will carry out such a blood test on the premises. If they do not keep the necessary equipment to hand, they will be forced to send the sample to be analysed at a laboratory, which will take time. If your stud owner insists on a 24-hour certificate you will need to find a vet able to complete the tests on his own premises.

Calling

As I have already discussed, most Persian queens are likely to start calling once they reach the age of 10 to 14 months. Each calling period will last about four or five days, and the queen will come into call at regular intervals during her reproductive life. Exactly how often she calls will depend on the individual, and be influenced by the time of the year. A queen will call much less frequently during the winter, especially if she is not kept indoors. Many queens will call regularly every three weeks, while some will call roughly every second month. In extreme cases, a queen may call almost every week, causing great strain both to the cat and her owner. In such cases she must be mated as soon as possible, neutered, or given a contraceptive to prevent her calling. (Contraceptive methods, however, may not be safe for a cat intended for breeding; your vet should be consulted about this.) A queen should not be allowed to call this frequently, as she is likely to lose her condition.

A queen on call can be very single-minded: all she can think about is finding a mate. Make sure she cannot escape the house during this period, or you may find she seeks out the local ginger tom as father to her kittens! Different queens call in different ways. Some may just miaow a little, rolling over onto their backs, purring and generally being more friendly than is usual. Others however may be incredibly loud, producing a very distinctive miaow capable of drowning out almost anything! When you touch her back or tail, she may groan and lie on her belly, thrusting her backside and tail up in the air, and each time she calls she is likely to become more obvious in her actions. Some queens will also "spray" urine over part of her living area, much like an un-neutered tom cat.

Taking the Queen to the Stud

As soon as you notice signs that your queen is on call, contact the stud owner and make arrangements to take her to the stud. It is best to get her there as soon as possible, on either the first or second day of call. If you wait any longer, the journey may put her off call, and you will have had a wasted trip. If she is put off even though you have made the journey on the first or second day there is still a chance she will come back into call after a day or so.

Before you take your queen to her stud, make sure she is perfectly healthy, and free of fleas. A bath may put her off call, so use a good flea spray instead, and comb her thoroughly with a flea comb to ensure she is not carrying unwelcome visitors! Do not use a flea treatment based on depositing a drop of liquid on the cat's neck, as her mate will grab hold of her neck and it could make him sick. Make sure that her ears are clean, and if her coat is very long, trim away the fur around the base of her tail to help the stud mate her.

When you take your queen to stud, do not forget her FeLV-negative certificate (and any others requested) as well as her vaccination certificate, and check whether the stud owner would like to see her registration certificate and pedigree.

When you first arrive at stud, the owner will probably want to check that your queen is healthy; then she will be placed in her own compartment next to the stud's pen, allowing the two cats to see and sniff each other, whilst keeping them apart. It is important they are separated for a while to give them time to get used to each other, otherwise the queen may become frightened and attack the stud. If your queen is a maiden, especially if she is kept as a household pet, do not be surprised if she is not mated at her first visit. It is quite natural for a queen used to living indoors to be worried if she is suddenly put outside in a pen with a stud she has never met. Under such circumstances she may not allow herself to be mated. You may have to bring your queen back the next time she is on call: her second visit is likely to be more successful as everything will be more familiar to her. Of course there are exceptions: when Blondie (my first queen) was brought to Bluey (her stud) she immediately fell in love with him and did not even notice the strange circumstances.

Mating

You will probably need to leave your queen with the stud for up to five days; the stud owner will contact you once a mating has occurred and when he feels your queen is ready to return home. Cats are unusual in that females will not ovulate until after mating, so it is important that your queen remains with the stud to be mated several times during a two or three day period. A male cat's penis is covered in small spikes which cause the queen pain when he withdraws after mating. She is likely to scream, and may turn on the stud violently, so it is vital the stud owner is on hand to supervise the proceedings.

Bringing Your Queen Home

On collecting your queen, you should be given a mating certificate stating when the queen was mated, when the kittens can be expected, and detailing the stud's pedigree.

After arriving home with your queen, make sure she has no access to other male cats: if she is still on call, mating will still be possible, and the result could be a single litter of kittens with different fathers!

For the first few weeks after mating, you should look after your queen in the normal way; but do not take her to any shows, and avoid altering her diet suddenly or introducing any other drastic change in lifestyle. You will not know whether or not she is pregnant for at least three weeks. If she is, she will "pink-up" at about this time, her nipples becoming pink and enlarged. It may be a good idea to check them before mating her, taking careful note of their usual appearance so that any changes are more obvious. Pinking-up is quite a reliable sign that a queen is expecting: only rarely will a queen undergo a false (phantom) pregnancy, displaying all the signs without being pregnant. Pregnant cats do not usually call (although some have a short call during pregnancy), so this also may indicate a successful mating.

A good vet will be able to discover whether your queen is pregnant by palpating her abdomen four to five weeks after mating. Do not attempt to do this yourself in case you damage the unborn kittens. If you prefer not to risk upsetting your queen with a trip to the vet, stay at home and let nature take its course. If she is pregnant, she will start to put on weight after five or six weeks, and eventually her pregnancy will become very obvious. She will probably sleep a lot, and will need to eat more than before.

The Pregnant Queen

Treat your pregnant queen with care. Handle her more carefully than usual, and make sure she does not jump or leap around too much once she begins to get bigger.

Check all medications (worming for example) before you give them, as some may be unsafe for pregnant queens or harmful to unborn kittens. Ideally your queen will have been wormed before mating. If she should fall ill, make sure your vet knows she is expecting, so that he can take her condition into account when prescribing any drugs.

About a week before the predicted due date you should clip some of the queen's coat, trimming the fur on her stomach so that her nipples are clearly visible. This will help the kittens suckle easily. Then clip away some of the fur at the base of her tail, and the top of her back legs, to stop it getting unnecessarily dirty and messy during the birth. It may also help to rub her nipples gently with some olive oil, leaving them softer and more supple.

Most cats are pregnant for 63 to 65 days, although kittens can arrive early, after about 60 days, or later, 70 days being more or less the limit. Do not worry if the kittens are overdue, as long as your queen remains fit and healthy.

Peace and quiet are essential during the last week of pregnancy, so you should keep any other household cats or dogs away from the mother-to-be. Your queen will need a safe place to live during this time, and in which to have her kittens. Make sure you put bowls of food and water and a litter tray where she can reach them, and provide a place where she can give birth. A soft cat bed (available in pet shops) or a cardboard box lined with newspapers or blankets will do. Remember to change the bedding once the kittens have been born. Alternatively you can buy a special "kittening box". Most queens will accept the place you offer, especially if you have introduced it in advance, but some are determined to choose their own site. If your cat does begin to give birth in an inconvenient place, let her finish before moving her and her new family to the site you have prepared.

If a queen is not kept on her own during this time she may become very disturbed; if she is forced to give birth in the presence of other cats she may even kill her kittens, so do be sure to isolate her.

If there is a "best" place for your queen to spend her last week of pregnancy and her first few weeks of motherhood, it is your bedroom. It is important that you are able to watch over her constantly, and are on hand to help should a problem occur. If you do not let your queen make her den in your bedroom, you may not be aware of any night-time crises.

A soft cat bed like this is ideal for the queen with her litter.
Photo - Nick Mays.

During pregnancy, your queen should be allowed to eat as much as she wants. She will probably ask for one or two extra meals a day. In the last three weeks of pregnancy, supplements of calcium and/or vitamins may do her good, and you should give her milk to drink. For advice, consult your vet. Bear in mind, however, that too much calcium can produce large kittens. If they are too big to be born naturally, your vet will be forced to perform a caesarian section.

The Birth

A pet cat will usually welcome your presence at the birth of her kittens, but you should not interfere unless it becomes absolutely vital.

A queen about to give birth will be restless for about an hour, sometimes miaowing all the while. Once her contractions start, she will seek a place to give birth - hopefully in the bed you have chosen for her. Once she is settled, the queen will strain for between 30 minutes and an hour before the first kitten appears. She will probably be squatting on her bed, and her contractions will be clearly visible. If she strains for more than an hour without producing a kitten you should call the vet.

Most kittens will appear head first, then quickly slide from their mother into the world. However it is not unusual for kittens to be born backwards, with their tails and hind-legs emerging first. This does not usually present a problem. If a kitten becomes stuck, you should help the queen by pulling the kitten gently, in time with her contractions. Be careful not to pull too hard, as this could damage the queen.

Kittens remain in their amniotic sac during birth, the placenta (or after-birth) attached to the kitten via the umbilical cord. The queen should remove the sac from the kitten's head immediately to prevent suffocation, but some queens, especially first-time mothers, may be unsure of what to do. If this is the case, then you must help. Tear the sac away and encourage the mother to lick her kitten. Newborn kittens should cry straight away, but if a kitten does not cry, or is not breathing, you must act quickly to save it. This problem is often caused by fluid in the lungs, so you should remove any fluid from the kitten's nostrils, and gently open its jaw and clean its mouth with your finger. Rub the kitten vigorously with a flannel or a towel. If it still does not breathe, hold it firmly in your hand, making sure you support its head, and swing it downwards through the air; alternatively, hold it upside down and pinch its feet to make it cry. If this fails to clear out the fluid, breathe very gently into its mouth until it starts crying, taking great care not to blow too hard, or you risk damaging its tiny lungs.

Once the kitten is crying, its mother should chew at the umbilical cord until it is severed. Again, if she fails to act you will have to help. Pinch the cord with your fingernails, pulling towards the kitten to cut the cord about an inch from the kitten's body. You should never pull the cord away from the kitten, as this could cause a hernia. A rough cut, from the mother's teeth or your fingernails, will bleed less than a clean cut with scissors.

Once the kitten is breathing and has had its cord cut, it should be put to the mother to suckle. The next kitten will probably appear 20 to 30 minutes after the first. A normal litter size for a first-time mother is about three or four kittens, but a queen can carry up to seven, sometimes even ten (although this is rare).

Once you are certain the queen has finished giving birth, let her settle down to suckle her kittens. Her bed will be dirty, but you should wait a few hours, or until she gets up to eat or use the litter tray, before replacing the soiled bedding with clean material. After the birth, offer your queen a drink of milk with an egg yolk stirred into it, as she will probably be very hungry and thirsty.

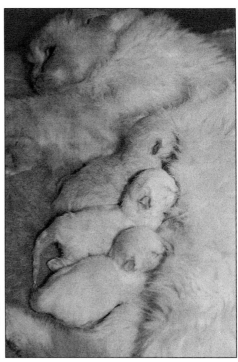

Each kitten will have its own nipple to suckle from, and this will hardly ever vary.
Photo - Nick Mays.

When to Call the Vet

Always call the vet if you suspect there is a problem during the birth. It is better to risk calling a vet unnecessarily than to put the lives of the queen and her kittens in jeopardy. Always call the vet if:

- the queen has been straining for more than an hour without producing a kitten, or if she strains for more than an hour after the birth of the last kitten.

- the queen seems unduly distressed.

- a kitten becomes stuck and you are unable to free it.

- if any afterbirth is retained. You should check carefully that a complete placenta emerges after each kitten has been born, as any which remains may cause infection. Some queens will eat the placenta, which is hormone-rich and will increase her milk supply.

A caesarian section may be necessary for a variety of reasons: a very large kitten may have become trapped, or one of the litter may be lying across the birth canal instead of along it. (It is worth noting that there is a slightly greater incidence of caesarian section births among Persians because their heads are larger on average than those of other breeds.) Queens suffering from similar one-off labour problems can be mated again without undue concern, but if your queen requires a caesarian because her birth canal is too narrow you should not continue to breed from her, as she will have the same problem next time around. In this case it would be wise to have her neutered at the time the caesarian is performed. The problem is often hereditary: any female kittens born of such a mother may suffer in the same way.

Kittens with Defects or Deformities

Most kittens are healthy and born without problems, but occasionally a kitten will be born with a defect or deformity.

Some kittens are born with a cleft palate: the bones in the roof of its mouth will not be joined together and as a result the kitten will not be able to suckle. Such a kitten will probably appear normal at birth, but eventually it will become obvious that the kitten is not getting any milk. If a kitten is hungry, it will cry a lot and move around. A kitten with a cleft palate may move from one nipple to the next without success; if you try to bottle-feed it, the kitten will make wheezing noises and milk will drip from its nose. Sadly there is no effective treatment for a kitten with a cleft palate: the only answer is to save it from suffering as early as possible and have it put to sleep humanely by a vet.

Sometimes kittens are born with their eyes open. A kitten's eyes are normally closed at birth, and remain closed for up to ten days. A kitten whose eyes are open at birth may suffer permanent eye damage. Make sure it is kept in a dimly lit room, preferably with the curtains drawn, and avoid exposing it to bright light. This should protect the kitten's eyes, reducing the risk of damage, and it is possible that the problem will correct itself and the eyes will close.

A kitten which keeps its eyes closed for too long may also suffer damaged eyes. If it has not opened its eyes after about 12 days, it will probably need help to do so. If after 10 or 12 days the eyes have not opened naturally, gently bathe the kitten's eyelids with cotton wool soaked in lukewarm water, or consult your vet.

A kitten born with a portion of its intestine, encased within a pouch of skin, protruding from its stomach is said to have an umbilical hernia. The condition can vary in severity, in extreme cases the whole of the kitten's intestines being housed outside its body, producing a large lump. Kittens born like this should be put to sleep by a vet. In less severe cases, only a small bump will be visible on the kitten's stomach and it will be possible to push the lump into the stomach. If the kitten is held on its back the lump will fall into place, disappearing from view. Kittens born in this state do not usually experience any problems, and can live a happy life. Surgery may be necessary as the cat grows older, however, and you should ask a vet to examine the kitten as early as possible. An umbilical hernia can be caused by the kitten's mother chewing off the umbilical cord too close to the kitten's body. More frequently the cause is hereditary, so it is unwise to breed from any cat with an umbilical hernia, no matter how slight the problem may be.

Persian kittens are sometimes born with "frog legs", or twisted hind legs, giving the hind legs an appearance of being the wrong way round. This is usually caused by a straightforward muscle problem, and can often be corrected with exercise. Make sure the kitten has a rough surface on which to walk without its hind legs slipping away from underneath its body: a towel is ideal. In rare cases, the kitten's bones may be deformed, so ask your vet to check any kitten born with frog legs.

Polydactyl kittens are born with extra digits, sometimes as many as double the normal five toes on each paw. This condition is more common in non-pedigree cats, but it does occur in pedigree Persians occasionally. It is not painful, but it is hereditary, so you should not breed from a polydactyl kitten.

Tail defects are common in most pedigree breeds. A kitten may have a slight bump or indentation at the tip of its tail. This could be so slight as to be unnoticeable for the first few weeks, or it may have a more obvious kink. Sometimes a kitten is born with only half its tail. Tail defects do not cause a cat problems, but they too are hereditary, and bar a cat from being used for breeding.

Hand Rearing Kittens

If you are very unlucky, you may find yourself with a litter of kittens and no mother to look after them. It might not be because your queen has died; she could simply be disinterested. A queen subjected to a caesarian may produce little or no milk, or she may simply feel too ill after her experience to be able to care for her newborn kittens. It will fall to you to make sure the kittens are feeding properly.

The first thing you should do in such a case is to make sure the kittens are kept warm. If the mother is unavailable, the best solution is to cover a soft cat bed with a blanket, under which you should put a heating pad to keep the kittens warm and cosy. Be careful not to let the pad get too hot: the lowest heat setting should be sufficient.

If possible, try to find a foster mother for the kittens. Another breeder in your area may have a queen with a litter of similar age who could perhaps foster them. The local RSPCA might be able to help, but do be sure that any queen drafted in as a foster mother has been blood-tested and is in good health.

If no foster mother can be found, you are left with no option but to hand-rear the kittens. This can be rewarding, but is very hard work, as newborn kittens will need to be fed every two hours, day and night. Suitable feeding bottles can be bought in pet shops, and your vet may be able to help; a syringe without the needle will sometimes do the trick. There are several milk substitutes available, and it is best to use a brand which has been specifically developed for cats. Follow the manufacturer's instructions very carefully. The kittens may be reluctant to drink from a bottle at first, but most will quickly get the hang of it. Try not to force the milk down the kitten's throat or you may choke it. If the milk bubbles out through the kitten's nostrils it is probably going down the wrong way: decrease the flow until the kitten is comfortable.

Offer the kitten as much as it wants - initially this will be about 2ml at each feed. As the kitten grows older, you will gradually be able to reduce the number of feeds, particularly at night. After about three weeks, begin to introduce solid food (eg baby rice) and mix it with the kitten's milk. (More details on weaning kittens are given in the section on kitten development.)

After each feed, you should imitate the ritual licking performed by a mother cat, by wiping the kitten with damp cotton wool or tissue, particularly around the tail area. This will make the kitten urinate. In the absence of a mother cat, who would wash them frequently, hand-reared kittens are likely to become very dirty, so it is important that you clean them regularly with a damp flannel.

The "Bigger Better Kitten" Syndrome

A form of rivalry can occur if two queens and their kittens share the same room. The mother with the younger litter may spot the older, larger kittens, and decide that because they are bigger, they must be better than her own. Consequently she will abandon her own kittens in favour of the older litter. If this happens, you should separate the two queens. Prevention is best, however: if you have the space, provide each queen with her own room in which to raise her litter.

Sexing Kittens

For a novice, the sexing of young kittens may seem difficult, but it is a skill soon learned with practice. Try to sex the kittens as early as possible, before the fur covering the genital area grows too long. A female kitten is distinct because the openings of her vagina and anus are very close together. A male kitten has a much larger space between his penis and anus, the penis area appearing larger and protruding more than the female's vaginal area.

Kitten Development

Kittens develop rapidly, and their progress is fascinating to follow. At birth, a Persian kitten will weigh between 60g and 150g, most usually about 100g ($3^1/_2$ oz). Providing they receive adequate nutrition, even the smallest of kittens can grow into large adult cats. One of my Persians, a neutered male called Bellhop, weighed only 80g at birth. Now an adult, he is the largest of all my cats. After birth, your kittens will probably put on weight at the rate of about 10g a day.

Proud mum, Ch Cheval Cherish (owned by Val Robinson of the Cheval Colourpoints), with her litter of three-day-old kittens.
Photo - Shaun Flannery.

Persian Cats

Colourpoint Persian kittens, three days old. The eyes and ears are closed, while the colour is essentially white - the coloured points do not develop until later. Photo - Shaun Flannery.

Three-day-old Persian kitten.
Photo - Shaun Flannery.

Weigh the kittens regularly to make sure they are growing properly. At about five weeks, each kitten should weigh about 500g. Within a day or so of birth, most kittens will purr audibly when suckling their mother. This is a good sign, indicating the kitten is happy and content. A hungry kitten will cry a lot and be restless. After four or five days, the stumps of the kittens' umbilical cords will have dried and fallen off. After about ten days, a kitten's ears will unfold, enabling it to hear, and at roughly the same time (often between 10 and 12 days in Persians) the eyes will open. At first, a slit in the eye will become visible; the eye will then open gradually over the next couple of days.

Once your kittens have opened their eyes, they will become much more alert and interested in what is going on around them. They will start to walk, wash themselves, and (at about three weeks of age) start play-fighting with each other. The kittens may be brave enough to venture outside the cat-bed for the first time at about this stage, walking carefully around the room to explore. However, they may not be quite up to climbing back in, and may need assistance from their mother - or from you!

From now on there will be no looking back. Their teeth will begin to show between three and four weeks of age, and soon after that weaning can begin. The kittens will need to continue suckling their mother for at least ten weeks, but solid food should also become an important part of their diet. I prefer to wean kittens on first-stage baby food, a meat flavour usually proving the most popular. Mix the baby food with some kitten milk, then offer it to the

The kittens are now three weeks old. They can see and hear, the long fur has started to grow and the darker points on their feet, tail, face and ears are starting to show.

Persian kittens are irresistable at this age...

... and just starting to move around.

At the age of three weeks, a Persian kitten is slightly bigger than a human hand...

... and at eight weeks it is a bigger handful!

Photos - Shaun Flannery.

kittens on your fingertips. They may take a day or two to get going, but soon they will be eating enthusiastically and are ready for solid meals up to five times a day. As soon as the kittens accept baby food with no problems, the time is ripe to switch to special kitten food (tinned is usually best). Try to stop them tucking into their mother's adult food, as it may upset their stomachs, and prevent the queen from stealing her kittens' food by removing her whilst the kittens are eating.

When the kittens reach five weeks of age, they will start to copy their mother in everything she does, including using the litter tray. Make sure the sides of your litter tray are low enough for the kittens to climb in. Almost all kittens will house-train themselves, and will not need to be taught cleanliness. Many kittens will have the occasional accident. When this happens, simply put the kitten in the litter tray and it will soon understand. The extent to which a kitten becomes litter-trained depends a great deal upon its mother: a clean mother will raise clean kittens.

Once the kittens begin to venture out and about, start grooming them. The more you handle them and get them used to people, the better. Do not invite too many visitors until the kittens have been vaccinated, however, as

viruses can be brought into the house on shoes. Kittens reared on their mother's milk will have some natural immunity, but it is wise to take a few precautions. When the kittens are able to move around with ease, let them emerge from the bedroom roughly once a day, so that they will become accustomed to the world around them, including household appliances like televisions and vacuum cleaners - and any other household pets!

This eight-week-old Colourpoint kitten is obviously used to being handled.
Photo - Shaun Flannery.

Eight-week-old kittens are full of mischief. Photo - Shaun Flannery.

Worm the kittens with a liquid kitten wormer when they are about eight weeks old, and repeat the treatment two weeks later. At nine weeks of age, it is time for their first vaccinations; the second injection is given at 12 weeks of age. At this stage the kittens will be ready to go to their new homes.

Registering Your Kittens

The GCCF will not permit registration of any kitten until at least one calendar month after its birth. In many cases it is wise to wait a couple of weeks longer to get a better idea which register (active or non-active) will best suit each kitten. Only good quality kittens worth breeding from should be registered as active. Any kitten you think is not up to breed standard (a kitten with a kinked tail, too long a face, or a colour fault, for example) should be placed on the non-active register. It should be possible to make a reasonably accurate assessment of a kitten's quality by the time it is six weeks old.

Registration forms on which to register your litter are available from the GCCF. Make sure you read the instructions carefully. If you already have a GCCF-registered prefix (like a "kennel" name) it will cost about £4 to register each kitten. Applications to register a prefix should be sent to the GCCF, and cost £50 (at 1996 prices). Registering kittens without a prefix is slightly more expensive, at about £6 per kitten.

If you do use a registered prefix, the names you choose for your kittens will automatically be unique, so you will not usually need to worry about selecting several alternatives as is the case if you have not adopted a prefix. If in doubt, refer carefully to the instructions on the form. The GCCF will add an administrative prefix to your chosen name. This will indicate in which year the kitten was registered, as the word chosen changes from year to year (Adkrilo: 1989, Adhuilo: 1990, or Adraylo: 1991, for example). You will find that Longhair cats will always be given an administrative prefix ending with the letters "lo", to identify their Longhair type.

Selling Your Kittens

Once your kittens are 12 weeks old and fully vaccinated, they are ready to leave for their new homes. By now you may well have succumbed to the temptation to keep one - or even two - but you will probably still have at least a couple to sell.

Finding homes for your kittens is a serious undertaking. It is not simply a question of parting with a kitten in exchange for money. Responsible breeders will make enquiries to ensure as far as possible that their kittens go to good homes, where they will be properly cared for throughout their lives. Do not expect it to be easy, especially if you are not yet established as a well known breeder. You will find that many people enquire, but only a small percentage of enquirers will buy a kitten.

If your litter has been bred from show-winning parents, other breeders will very probably be interested. It is a good idea to spread the word by placing an advertisement in your Persian breed club's membership journal, or in any other cat club journal, either before or just after the litter arrives. Once the kittens have been born, it will be possible to announce their arrival in *Cat World* magazine's Register of Births.

A prospective buyer in search of a good quality kitten will not mind waiting until the kittens are 12 weeks old and ready to leave home.

However, it is not usually worth advertising your kittens elsewhere until they are older, and almost ready to leave home, as the general reader-ship interested in buying a pedigree kitten as a pet tends to have less patience. At this stage, try an advertise-ment in the various cat magazines and in your local newspaper.

These kittens are now 12 weeks old, fully weaned and ready to leave for their new homes. Photo - Shaun Flannery.

Persian Cats

Do try to establish that a prospective buyer will make a suitable owner. Does he (or she) realise how much grooming the cat will need? Is he aware of how he will need to pay for annual vaccinations and occasional veterinary bills? Does he understand about neutering, worming, de-fleaing.... A kitten is not a toy to be discarded once the novelty has worn off: the new owner must be prepared to look after it for its natural life. Ask all the questions you consider necessary. Genuine buyers understand that you are enquiring out of genuine concern for your kittens.

You may like to consider writing and signing a "contract" stating whether the kitten was purchased as a pet, breeding animal or show animal. You could add a clause offering you, as the cat's breeder, first refusal of the cat (or the opportunity to find it a new home) should the new owner find that for some reason he has to part with it in the future. Some cat clubs will supply specimen contracts, and the GCCF has prepared a standard form for use when selling pet kittens intended neither for breeding nor showing.

Price your kittens with care. A show quality kitten should be sold at a higher price than a pet quality kitten, and it is important to get the balance right: avoid under or over-pricing. Ask around to discover what other breeders charge for their pedigree kittens. I would not recommend charging less than £125 each for pet quality kittens: they are pedigree cats, and it will have cost you a considerable amount to rear them. Cheap kittens may attract the wrong type of buyer, only interested because of the low price.

Once you have decided on a price, stick to it and do not be tempted to waver. Insist on a non-returnable deposit, usually between 10 and 20% of the total price, if a buyer wishes to reserve a kitten in advance. Under no circumstances should you hand over the kitten's pedigree and registration papers until you have been paid in full.

It is also a good idea to take an insurance policy to cover your kittens for the first four to six weeks in their new homes. This can cost as little as £5 or £10. Check with several pet insurance specialists for the best deal.

Finally, be sure to tell your kittens' new owners what they are used to eating, and try to give the new owners enough of the food to last each kitten for a few days. Do not forget to ask the new owner to telephone you to let you know how the kitten is getting on in its new home. I can guarantee that it will be heart-breaking to sell your precious kittens, even if have decided to keep one back, and you will want to be sure they have settled in well.

Colour Breeding

Colour breeding is very complex, requiring a knowledge of genetics to mate the right colours and produce an acceptably coloured pedigree Persian cat. A Colourpoint mated to a Black Smoke, for example, will probably produce pretty offspring, but the kittens will not be eligible for registration on the active register. Because of its complexity, this topic cannot properly be covered in a book of this size. For more information, contact your breed club (which may be able to supply colour mating charts outlining the probable results of various matings) and to specialist books on the subject.

Three-week-old Seal Point Colourpoint Persian kitten.
Photo - Nick Mays.

11

ailments

A healthy cat will usually live for 13 to 15 years, perhaps even longer. Pedigree cats are sometimes a little more sensitive than non-pedigrees, and may be more prone to disease, but most Persians live to a great age with no health problems whatsoever. It is important, however, to take your cat to the vet for annual booster inoculations and health checks.

Listed here are some of the more common diseases and health problems which may affect cats, along with the appropriate treatment. This list is only intended as a general guide. If you are in any doubt about your cat's health, consult a veterinary surgeon (veterinarian) as soon as possible. It is as well to be aware of the symptoms and this list may be helpful, but do remember that most cats, like most people, are fit and well for the majority of their lives.

Diarrhoea

Symptoms: The cat's motions (faeces) are softer than usual, sometimes liquid, and smell offensive. The cat's behaviour depends on the cause of the diarrhoea, and upon the severity of its condition. Many cats with diarrhoea appear to be perfectly healthy, and still want to eat, but most will go to the toilet more frequently, and may do so in unusual places (other than the litter tray). Persian cats with diarrhoea will almost always have faeces matted in the fur underneath the tail and around the hind-legs. It is very important to keep this area clean, especially in the summer, to prevent infestations of maggots. Cats with severe diarrhoea, or with another disease as an underlying cause, may strain when passing motions, and appear generally unwell, perhaps refusing to eat. Sometimes blood can be seen in the motions.

Causes: Several. Many Persian cats are sensitive to cows' milk, and this may lead to diarrhoea.

Other possible causes include changes in the diet (a new brand of food, for example), excessive eating, infections, parasites, and other diseases such as Feline Enteritis.

Treatment: Provided that the cat appears healthy in other respects, starve it for 24 hours to allow its stomach to settle. (The cat should have access to clean drinking water at all times.) If the cat has not passed any motions after 24 hours' starvation, or if its motions appear firmer, a small amount of boiled chicken can be given. Feed only about a quarter of the amount the cat would normally eat in a day, and gradually increase the amount of chicken, until the cat's motions are normal. When the motions have been normal for about three days, gradually introduce the cat's usual diet by mixing it a spoonful at a time with the chicken.

Should the diarrhoea persist for more than 24 hours, consult your vet. Should the diarrhoea be accompanied by other symptoms such as vomiting or lethargy, see a vet immediately. Do not ignore diarrhoea, as if it is not treated it will eventually lead to dehydration.

Constipation

Symptoms: The cat strains when going to the toilet, passing either a small quantity of very hard motions, no motions at all, or some liquid which may be mistaken for diarrhoea. A cat with constipation may refuse to eat, and will often be lethargic. In severe cases, the cat may even start to vomit as it absorbs toxins from the constipated motions retained in the bowel.

Causes: Several, including fur-balls in the stomach; a collection of debris after eating bones and/or bird feathers; or as a result of nerve-damage caused by an accident.

Treatment: In simple cases it is usually enough to give the cat a dose of two to five millilitres of medicinal paraffin oil (one half to one teaspoonful). If the cat is reluctant to take the oil (most cats like the taste) pour the oil sideways into the cat's mouth with a spoon, or with an eye-dropper or syringe. Do not pour the oil into the cat's mouth from the front - under the nose - as this will make the cat choke.

If this treatment does not help, or if the cat appears otherwise to be unwell, consult a vet.

Ear Infection (Otitis Externa)

Symptoms: The cat scratches one or both ears, and may also shake its head. If the cat is scratching excessively, the fur behind its ears may be missing, and the skin will become sore. The ear will smell, and sometimes produce a visible discharge, either brown and waxy, or of a paler colour and pus-like. In Persians, the discharge will often mat the long fur underneath the cat's ears. The inside of the ear may look inflamed.

Causes: Several, including fight wounds; foreign bodies such as grass seeds in the ear; ear mites. It can also be caused by over-zealous cleaning of the cat's ears, or by an overproduction of wax.

Treatment: Carefully clean the ear with damp cotton buds. Remove any visible foreign bodies. If the cause is not apparent, consult a vet who is likely to prescribe eardrops.

Ear Mites

Symptoms: The cat will scratch its ears vigorously, often causing the inside of the ears to bleed, and will probably shake its head. A large amount of dark, almost black, discharge can be seen inside the ear.

Cause: A mite called *Otodectes Cynotis*, which lives in the ear canal. Ear mites are common in outdoor cats, and especially in kittens, but rare in pedigree cats with limited or no outdoor access. They usually spread from one cat to another.

Treatment: Ear drops prescribed by a vet. The drops should be inserted into the ear canal at least once daily for two weeks. Once the crusty discharge has started to soften, the ears must be cleaned thoroughly every day with cotton wool. The cat's ear canal bends at the far end, so the ear may still be clogged by discharge in that part of the canal which you cannot reach even when the ear has been cleaned and looks clear. When the cat shakes its head, more discharge will appear. It is important to continue the treatment for as long as any discharge remains. If there are other cats or dogs in the household, they may need treating as well to contain cross-infection.

Aural Haematoma

Symptoms: Swelling of the cat's ear flap, causing the appearance of a lump. Alternatively the whole ear may be swollen.

Cause: A blood blister: an enclosed swelling of the ear flap containing blood produced after the rupture of a blood vessel in the ear. This may be caused by excessive shaking of the head or scratching of the ears (often as a result of an ear infection or ear mites). It could be the result of a bite sustained during a fight with another cat.

Treatment: If the haematoma is small, it may help to rub an ice-cube against the swelling for a few minutes at a time, a couple of times a day. This will stop the internal bleeding, and may reduce the swelling. If this does not help, or if the swelling is large, consult a vet. The vet will drain the ear under anaesthetic, then stitch the wound. If a haematoma is left untreated, the swelling will eventually become hard and fibrous, and the ear will contract, distorting its shape, a condition often referred to as "cauliflower ear".

Feline Urological Syndrome (FUS)

This is a fairly common condition, both in male and female cats. It should always be treated as serious, as the condition can occasionally be fatal, especially in male cats. FUS consists of an inflammation caused by sand- or grit-like crystals in the cat's urine. In male cats the urethra is long, narrow and contains a bend which can easily become blocked. In females, the urethra is shorter and broader, and very rarely becomes blocked.

Symptoms: The cat squats frequently, and strains without managing to urinate. It will probably lick its penis or vulva. If the cat does manage to pass small amounts of urine, it will do so frequently, sometimes in places it would not normally urinate. Blood may be present in the urine. In males whose urethra is partially or completely blocked, the cat may cry in pain when handled, appear lethargic with a swollen abdomen, and sometimes the penis will protrude, showing a red and swollen tip.

Causes: Several, or a combination of factors, including infections; too much magnesium in the cat's diet; not enough water to drink; too much dry food; and reduced physical activity. If the cat's access to the place in which it normally urinates is restricted (if it is in a strange place, for example) it may hold its urine for a long period, retaining stale urine in its bladder, and this can be harmful.

Treatment: Consult a vet as soon as possible. If treatment is delayed, the cat may die because of the build up of toxic waste products in the blood, or because of a ruptured bladder. The vet will put the cat under anaesthetic and clear the blockage. Afterwards, the cat will receive medication. If a cat repeatedly suffers, surgery to shorten the male urethra can be performed. Special prescription diets are also available from vets.

Cystitis

This is an inflammation of the bladder, which is often associated with FUS (see above) in male cats. In females, it is caused by FUS or a bacterial contamination of the vulva.

Symptoms: The cat will urinate more frequently than normal, often in unusual places. It will probably lick its genital area, and the small amounts of urine it passes may be tinged with blood.

Cause: If the cat refrains from urinating for a lengthy period, such as may occur if it is removed from its usual urinating place, stale urine retained in the bladder will provide a good breeding ground for bacteria.

Treatment: Consult a vet - he will test the urine, and prescribe appropriate antibiotics. Make sure that the cat has plenty to drink. In some cases cystitis may be caused by a tumour or stones in the bladder. An X-ray will show whether this is the case.

Gingivitis

Symptoms: The cat's gums will be red and inflamed, especially along the tooth-gum margin. The cat will probably have bad breath, and may drool. The gums may bleed when touched and in bad cases the cat may show interest in food but be reluctant to eat.

Causes: Several, including tartar on the teeth; infections; excessive vitamin A intake; or irritant substances licked from the cat's coat.

Treatment: Consult a vet who will prescribe antibiotics. If necessary, the cat will be put under anaesthetic to allow the removal of tartar, and the extraction of any unhealthy teeth. (It is important to prevent a build-up of tartar on your cat's teeth. If the tartar is removed frequently every two to three months (as soon as the substance appears) the cat should never suffer from a heavy build-up, and therefore avoid the need for anaesthetic for this purpose. Tartar can be removed fairly easily using a dentist's tooth scraper. If you get your cat used to this treatment from an early age, it should not pose too much of a problem.)

Kidney Disease

Cats have two kidneys which filter waste products from the bloodstream. If the kidneys are not functioning properly, the waste products which accumulate in the bloodstream may have a toxic or poisoning effect on the cat, which can eventually be fatal. There are two main types of kidney disease, chronic and acute. Chronic kidney disease is common in older cats over the age of nine years.

Acute Kidney Disease

Symptoms: The cat will not eat, despite showing an interest in food. It will often drink more than usual, though in some cases it could drink less. It will vomit, be lethargic, and gradually become dehydrated. Its coat will appear rough and unkempt because the cat will stop grooming itself.

Cause: Most often seen in younger cats, up to six years of age. It is distinguished from chronic kidney disease by its sudden onset and very obvious symptoms. Causes vary, but include infections; accidents leading to kidney damage; poisoning; other diseases.

Treatment: Consult a vet who will diagnose the disease by a blood test. A dehydrated cat may need to remain at the vet's surgery during treatment. Once the cat has started to recover, it is important to feed a balanced diet which will not strain the kidneys - special diets are available from vets.

Chronic Kidney Disease

Symptoms: The cat will drink more than usual, and consequently urinate more frequently. It will lose weight, and may be lethargic. Its coat will be rough because the cat will stop grooming itself. The cat will vomit occasionally, and will probably suffer from bad breath. Because a cat will often appear healthy for long periods, chronic kidney disease can be difficult to spot. Look out for the signs of increased drinking and occasional vomiting.

Cause: The disease is common in older cats, and often develops slowly. It may be months, or even years, before a cat's owner realises the cat is ill. Possible causes include infections, other diseases and cystic kidneys; the specific cause often remains unidentified.

Treatment: Consult a vet, who will be able to confirm the disease after blood tests and urine samples. Medication including antibiotics and steroids may be given, and the cat's diet should be altered. Special kidney-friendly diets are available from vets. On a suitable diet, many cats with chronic kidney disease live happily for years.

Dehydration

Symptoms: To check whether a cat is dehydrated, pinch and lift the skin at the back of its neck. When you release it, the skin should fall back into place quickly. If it moves only slowly, or stays in a pinched position, the cat is dehydrated.

Causes: Several, often a result of severe diarrhoea.

Treatment: Consult a vet as soon as possible.

Ringworm

This is a fungus which affects the skin. Ringworm is every cat breeder's nightmare, because it is extremely contagious. It affects not only cats, but also other animals and humans. If you suspect ringworm in your household, it is essential you and your cat do not mix with other cats or visit shows. (Contact the GCCF for an advice leaflet.) Ringworm spores may also be carried by paper, so you should be careful not to write to people who keep cats.

Symptoms: Characteristic circular, irregular or diffuse areas of hair loss. These may be from a half to two-and-a-half centimetres in diameter, and the centre of the area will be clear. In humans, irritating red circles appear on various parts of the body. In cats, most circles appear around the head. Approximately two weeks will lapse between contact with the fungus and the appearance of the lesions. To confirm the disease a vet will either use Wood's Lamp (an ultra-violet light under which infected areas appear green in colour) or send skin scrapings and hair samples for laboratory testing.

Cause: Fungus, spread either by direct or indirect contact. The fungus lives on hair, and can therefore be caught from loose hairs, infected brushes and combs etc.

Treatment: Consult a vet as soon as possible. The cat will be given fungus medication in the form of tablets, and will require regular bathing in special treatments. Carefully clean the whole house to remove any spores that may still be present.

Miliary Eczema

Symptoms: Thinning of the hair, possibly accompanied by scaly skin.

Cause: Several: may be caused by a flea allergy; vitamin B deficiency; endocrine disorder (particularly in neutered cats).

Treatment: Consult a vet. The usual treatment is with progesterone-like drugs, given orally. In some cases the cat will need maintenance doses of the drug over a long period of time.

Vomiting

Causes: Several. Bear in mind that cats will sometimes vomit for no obvious reason, simply regurgitating food. This may not necessarily be a sign of ill-health. However, if it happens more than four times in a 24-hour period, something may be wrong. The cause may be foreign materials in the stomach (grass or a bone); fur-balls in the stomach; infections; worms; severe constipation; travel sickness; over eating; or sensitivity to food.

Treatment: Cats will eat grass to make themselves vomit, thereby cleaning out the stomach. Occasional eating of grass and consequent vomiting is acceptable and no treatment is needed. Fur-balls form when the cat grooms itself and swallows fur. The fur will eventually accumulate in the stomach, and is often vomited up in sausage-like shapes. This, too, is perfectly normal, and nothing to worry about. If the cat vomits immediately after eating, without bringing up anything in particular, there may an object lodged in its stomach (a large fur-ball or a bone perhaps) which needs to be removed. In such cases, consult your vet. Cats suffering from frequent fur-balls will benefit from increased grooming to remove loose hairs.

If there is an obstruction in the stomach, the cat will vomit frequently and show signs of abdominal pain. Consult your vet as soon as possible - surgical removal may be the only solution.

If in addition the cat refuses to eat, and becomes lethargic, consult a vet immediately, as this may indicate a number of infections.

In the case of worms or travel sickness, consult a vet who will prescribe suitable medication.

Some greedy cats will vomit simply as a result of over-eating. In such cases, split the cat's meals into several smaller ones, and serve the food at room temperature rather than straight from the refrigerator.

Worms

Adult pedigree cats brought up indoors seldom contract worms. Worms are more common in cats allowed outdoor access, especially in cats which catch and eat prey such as mice and birds. For safety, it is recommended all cats are wormed regularly. Worm indoor cats twice a year; outdoor cats will need more frequent treatment.

Cats usually suffer from one of two types of worms: roundworms and tapeworms.

- **Roundworms** (3-10cm long) are slender, with tapered ends. To eradicate them, the cat must be wormed at least twice, leaving an interval of 10 to 14 days between treatment. Roundworms are usually present in newborn kittens, so regular worming is essential during the first six months of life.

- Usually only the segments of a **tapeworm** will be visible: they look like grains of rice (0.5-1cm long) and are flatter than roundworms. Tapeworms can be contracted by the cat ingesting fleas when it licks itself, so adequate flea control is important.

Symptoms: weight loss; pot-bellied appearance; dull coat; poor appetite; diarrhoea; appearance of a "third eyelid" across the cat's eyes. In severe cases, worms can be seen in the cat's faeces.

Treatment: Ask your vet for suitable worming pills, as wormers available from a veterinary surgeon are usually more effective, and produce fewer side effects, than those bought over the counter in chemists or pet shops.

Toxoplasmosis

Symptoms: The majority of infected cats show no symptoms at all. When they do occur, symptoms in kittens include high temperature; rapid breathing; diarrhoea; and sometimes death. Adult symptoms include weight loss; diarrhoea; unsteadiness; pale gums; possibly blindness.

Cause: A single cell parasite, *Toxoplasma gondii*. The disease is common in cats, and can be transferred to humans. There is added health risk to pregnant women, as it can harm the unborn child. Pregnant women should avoid cleaning out litter trays, as the disease may be contracted from infected faeces. (It may also be contracted from unwashed vegetables and raw meat.) Cats usually become infected after eating infected animals including birds and rodents. Kittens may be infected by the mother.

Treatment: Consult a vet who will test the cat's blood and faeces. The disease can be treated with antibiotics, but you should also try to prevent it by never feeding raw meat unless it has previously been frozen, and discouraging your cat from hunting.

Fleas

Almost all cats will suffer from fleas at least once during their lives. Fleas are common in Persians; they seem particularly attracted to long fur. Complete eradication is difficult, especially during the summer months, but you should do everything possible to keep the infestation under control. Fleas are very irritating for cats (some of which will be allergic to flea bites) and fleas help to spread tapeworm.

Cat fleas can be clearly seen. Before feeding on the cat's blood they are small and black in colour; after biting the cat they increase in size, and the blood they have ingested makes them appear browner. Fleas move very quickly, and can jump great distances, easily hiding in the long fur between jumps. A sure sign of a flea infestation will be the droppings they leave behind - small specks of black dirt. If the droppings come into contact with water they dissolve and become red in colour, as they consist mainly of dried blood. A flea comb is an absolute must for every owner of Persians, as it is the easiest method of removing flea dirt from the cat's coat, short of bathing.

Many methods of control are available, including the numerous flea sprays currently on the market, flea powders, pour-ons and flea collars. Some of these are good, others less effective. A good flea spray is probably the best way of killing fleas. Ask your vet to recommend one. You will need to spray regularly, about every 14 days. Kittens must be treated with great care. Kittens less than eight weeks are usually treated with special powder, although some sprays are suitable from four weeks. Follow the manufacturer's instructions carefully.

Flea collars are not recommended for Persian cats, as they wear away the fur around the neck. Some cats may also be sensitive to the collars, and may suffer from skin irritations.

In addition to treating your cat for fleas, you should also treat the cat's environment: your home. Fleas can live in carpets for several months. Special carpet and furniture sprays are available. Note that these should never be used on animals! "Flea traps" which attract and kill fleas living in carpets or furniture are also available.

New flea treatments are being developed all the time, so ask your vet for up-to-date advice.

Deafness

Cause: Deafness in cats is often an inherited problem, most commonly seen in blue-eyed white cats. Breeders should take care not to breed from deaf cats. Odd-eyed white cats may be deaf only in one ear, that ear being on the same side as the blue eye. Other causes of deafness may include infections, old age and blocked ear canals.

Treatment: Consult your vet. If the deafness is caused by a blockage or infection, treatment will be possible. Inherited deafness cannot be cured, and the cat will have to make the best of it. Most will learn to adapt to a life without hearing, especially if they were born deaf. Do not allow a deaf cat to venture outside, as it will be more vulnerable than a hearing cat.

Blocked Tear Ducts

Symptoms: The cat's eyes will be very runny, with copious tears streaming from the inner corners. This is common in Persians even without blocked tear ducts, so you may not need to take action. If the tear ducts are clear, similar discharge will run from the cat's eyes and nostrils. If the ducts are blocked, however, liquid will stream only from the eyes.

Cause: Persian cats are prone to this condition because of their flattened faces. The tear ducts may be squashed, narrow, or kinked, making it difficult for tears to flow freely.

Treatment: Consult a vet, who will be able to unblock the tear ducts under general anaesthetic.

Cataract

Symptoms: The lens of the eye gradually becomes white, and the cat's vision will deteriorate. A cataract may occur in one or both eyes.

Cause: Clouding of the eye's lens. Cataracts will eventually lead to blindness. They may occur in old age; after an injury or infection; or as a result of diabetes. They can also be inherited, so you should never breed from a cat with cataracts.

Treatment: Surgery may sometimes help.

Conjunctivitis

Symptoms: The eye becomes red and swollen, producing large amounts of clear or pus-like discharge.

Causes: Several, including foreign body in eye; injury; infection; allergy.

Treatment: Consult a vet, who will establish the cause then prescribe eye drops and/or ointment.

Feline Viral Rhinotracheitis (FVR)

Symptoms: The cat has an above-normal temperature (normal = 38.5°C) and becomes lethargic. It will sneeze and produce discharge from the nose and eyes. The eyes may be inflamed. The cat will probably refuse to eat, may drool and cough, and will eventually lose weight and become dehydrated.

Cause: Herpes virus. It is highly contagious, and can be spread either by direct or indirect contact. Can be prevented by vaccination.

Treatment: Consult a vet as soon as possible. He will prescribe antibiotics. An untreated cat will probably die. On recovery, some cats are left with a chronic sinus problem. Clean the cat's eyes and nostrils to make it more comfortable, isolate it from other cats, and encourage it to eat by offering its favourite foods. An infected cat will be reluctant to eat, as its blocked nostrils cause a reduction in its sense of smell. Warming the food may make it more interesting and attractive.

Feline Calici Virus (FCV)

Symptoms: Temperature rise, lethargy, and a poor appetite. The cat will have a clear discharge from its eyes and nose, and will probably dribble because of ulcers on its tongue. FCV can be fatal.

Cause: Virus spread either by direct or indirect contact.

Treatment: Consult a vet as soon as possible. The treatment is as for FVR. FVR and FCV are collectively known as Feline Influenza (Cat Flu), and can occur simultaneously. You should have your cat vaccinated against the two viruses.

Feline Infectious Enteritis or Feline Panleucopenia

Symptoms: Diarrhoea and vomiting, accompanied by fluctuating temperature and lethargy. The cat will soon become dehydrated, and probably experience abdominal pain.

Cause: Extremely contagious virus, usually fatal: about 90% of all young cats affected by this disease will die, some within 24 hours, often without exhibiting any symptoms. You should guard against the disease by vaccination. The virus is spread directly through contact with an infected cat, and indirectly by contact with infected faeces or bodily fluids.

Treatment: Consult your vet as soon as possible. Unfortunately the outcome is usually death, so vaccination is vital. The course usually starts when the kitten is about nine weeks, and consists of two initial injections and an annual booster.

Feline Leukaemia Virus (FeLV)

Symptoms: FeLV is generally considered a disease of the blood cells, but most often FeLV causes cancer of the lymphatic system, and may also involve other organs. Symptoms vary depending on the type of leukaemia. They may include poor appetite and weight loss; vomiting with diarrhoea; breathing problems; lethargy; and weakness. Queens exhibit further symptoms: infertility or miscarriage, or giving birth to dead or sickly kittens. Some cats which have contracted the virus will develop the symptoms, then become ill and die; others will recover, a small number becoming symptomless carriers.

Cause: A virus passed on from infected cats via the sharing of litter trays; food bowls; communal washing; bite wounds; contact with infected cats' faeces.

Treatment: Blood tests reveal the disease, so all cats intended for breeding should be tested regularly. The GCCF recommends the testing of all cats, whether or not you intend to breed. A single positive test may not be a certain indication of FeLV. The results of two tests taken at an interval of three months are more reliable.

If the second test is also positive your cat is likely to develop symptoms, and will probably die within a couple of years. Any cat with positive results will pose a health risk to other cats.

FeLV cannot be treated, but a vaccine is now available - ask your vet for advice.

Feline Infectious Peritonitis (FIP)

Symptoms: Poor appetite; weight loss; lethargy. The cat's stomach may swell, or breathing problems may develop, depending on the part of the body which is affected. Cats with FIP usually die within six weeks.

Cause: A virus, said to be more common in young cats.

Treatment: None available, neither has a vaccine been developed. Sick cats suspected of suffering from FIP can be blood-tested to discover whether they could be suffering from it. However, the only truly accurate means of diagnosis is by post mortem.

Feline Immunodeficiency Virus (FIV)

Symptoms: Poor appetite and weight loss; fluctuating temperature; swollen glands. The cat may be chronically unwell, perhaps with diarrhoea, mouth infections or breathing problems.

Cause: This virus is basically the same as the human HIV, but is species specific. This means that only cats can be affected; it will not affect other animals or humans. The virus is spread mainly by biting. As the immune system fails, other diseases may result.

Treatment: Consult a vet, who will conduct a blood test to confirm the disease. No treatment is available. As infected cats can live for years, presenting a health risk to others, they should either be housed in a single-cat household and denied outdoor access or be put to sleep.

Feline Acne

Symptoms: Irritated skin, usually on the cat's chin and lower lip.

Cause: Excess oils and dirt blocking the pores in the skin, causing pimples and small abscesses, similar to acne in humans.

Treatment: Consult a vet, who will prescribe an ointment, and perhaps also antibiotics.

Anal Gland Infections

Symptoms: The cat licks its anus, and may lose fur around the tail base area and on the inside of the hind-legs. Some cats seem unable to pinpoint the irritation, and will lick a large area, including the stomach. There will be fur loss, but the skin underneath will be healthy.

Cause: The cat has two small glands, one each side of its anus. These are scent glands, which produce a foul smelling liquid. This liquid is usually pressed out when the cat passes motions, or the cat may empty the glands when frightened. The glands sometimes become blocked. The cause is usually infrequent emptying, sometimes because of diarrhoea.

Treatment: Consult a vet, who will be able to empty the glands. Antibiotics may be prescribed if the glands are badly infected.

Abscesses

Symptoms: In the early stages, the swelling will probably be small and difficult to detect. As the abscess matures, it will form a larger bump, and will become less painful to the cat.

Cause: Usually a fight with another cat. Puncture wounds caused by a feline tooth can be very small and remain unnoticed until a swelling develops and the cat recoils from your touch.

Treatment: A vet will drain the abscess, probably under anaesthetic, and prescribe antibiotics.

Skin Cancer

Symptoms: The first signs are reddening and soreness of the edges of a cat's ears. The fur on the ears will fall out, and eventually the ears will become hairless and permanently red. This process may take years, and the cat will probably improve during the winter. Eventually the ears may curl, the skin will flake off and become itchy, and the ears will bleed easily.

Cause: Cats with white or very pale ears are prone to sunburn in the summer. This is because they lack protective skin pigmentation. If the cat spends a lot of time in the sun, the ears may become burnt, leading eventually to skin cancer of the ears.

Treatment: Consult a vet. Ear amputation may be necessary. To prevent this, apply a sun cream to the cat's ears, or discourage it from spending too long in the sun.

Cancer

Growths may be found on various parts of the body. These are usually benign growths which your vet can easily remove. Those found on the cat's mammary glands can be more serious, however, and veterinary advice should be sought as soon as they are discovered.

Euthanasia

All owners who love their cats are bound to be very upset when the time comes to say goodbye forever, but there is no reason to fear the experience of having a vet put the cat to sleep. The vet will simply give your cat an injection directly into a vein on one of its forelegs, and the cat will gently fall asleep within seconds, never to wake up again. It is a quick and painless process, and the cat will not have time to realise what is happening. A very nervous cat may be given a sedative first.

useful
addresses

THE GOVERNING COUNCIL OF THE CAT FANCY (GCCF)
4-6 Penel Orlieu
Bridgwater
Somerset
TA6 3PG   Tel: 01278-427575

CATS MAGAZINE
5 James Leigh Street
Manchester
M1 5NF   Tel: 0161-263 0577
(This is the official journal of the GCCF)

CAT WORLD MAGAZINE and SHOW CATS
10 Western Road
Shoreham-by-Sea
West Sussex
BN43 5WD   Tel: 01273-462000

YOUR CAT MAGAZINE
Bretton Court
Bretton
Peterborough
PE3 8DZ   Tel: 01733-264666

ALL ABOUT CATS MAGAZINE
Gong Publishing Group Limited
Suite C
21 Heathmans Road
London
SW6 4GP   Tel: 0171-384 3261

Persian Cats kittening chart

Based on a gestation period of 65 days

Mate	JAN	01	02	03	04	05	06	07	08	09	10	11	12	13	14	15
Kitten	MAR	07	08	09	10	11	12	13	14	15	16	17	18	19	20	21
Mate	FEB	01	02	03	04	05	06	07	08	09	10	11	12	13	14	15
Kitten	APR	07	08	09	10	11	12	13	14	15	16	17	18	19	20	21
Mate	MAR	01	02	03	04	05	06	07	08	09	10	11	12	13	14	15
Kitten	MAY	05	06	07	08	09	10	11	12	13	14	15	16	17	18	19
Mate	APR	01	02	03	04	05	06	07	08	09	10	11	12	13	14	15
Kitten	JUN	05	06	07	08	09	10	11	12	13	14	15	16	17	18	19
Mate	MAY	01	02	03	04	05	06	07	08	09	10	11	12	13	14	15
Kitten	JUL	05	06	07	08	09	10	11	12	13	14	15	16	17	18	19
Mate	JUN	01	02	03	04	05	06	07	08	09	10	11	12	13	14	15
Kitten	AUG	05	06	07	08	09	10	11	12	13	14	15	16	17	18	19
Mate	JUL	01	02	03	04	05	06	07	08	09	10	11	12	13	14	15
Kitten	SEP	04	05	06	07	08	09	10	11	12	13	14	15	16	17	18
Mate	AUG	01	02	03	04	05	06	07	08	09	10	11	12	13	14	15
Kitten	OCT	05	06	07	08	09	10	11	12	13	14	15	16	17	18	19
Mate	SEP	01	02	03	04	05	06	07	08	09	10	11	12	13	14	15
Kitten	NOV	05	06	07	08	09	10	11	12	13	14	15	16	17	18	19
Mate	OCT	01	02	03	04	05	06	07	08	09	10	11	12	13	14	15
Kitten	DEC	05	06	07	08	09	10	11	12	13	14	15	16	17	18	19
Mate	NOV	01	02	03	04	05	06	07	08	09	10	11	12	13	14	15
Kitten	JAN	05	06	07	08	09	10	11	12	13	14	15	16	17	18	19
Mate	DEC	01	02	03	04	05	06	07	08	09	10	11	12	13	14	15
Kitten	FEB	04	05	06	07	08	09	10	11	12	13	14	15	16	17	18

16	17	18	19	20	21	22	23	24	25	26	27	28	29	30	31	JAN
22	23	24	25	26	27	28	29	30	31	01	02	03	04	05	06	APR
16	17	18	19	20	21	22	23	24	25	26	27	28				FEB
22	23	24	25	26	27	28	29	30	01	02	03	04				MAY
16	17	18	19	20	21	22	23	24	25	26	27	28	29	30	31	MAR
20	21	22	23	24	25	26	27	28	29	30	31	01	02	03	04	JUN
16	17	18	19	20	21	22	23	24	25	26	27	28	29	30		APR
20	21	22	23	24	25	26	27	28	29	30	01	02	03	04		JUL
16	17	18	19	20	21	22	23	24	25	26	27	28	29	30	31	MAY
20	21	22	23	24	25	26	27	28	29	30	31	01	02	03	04	AUG
16	17	18	19	20	21	22	23	24	25	26	27	28	29	30		JUN
20	21	22	23	24	25	26	27	28	29	30	31	01	02	03		SEP
16	17	18	19	20	21	22	23	24	25	26	27	28	29	30	31	JUL
19	20	21	22	23	24	25	26	27	28	29	30	01	02	03	04	OCT
16	17	18	19	20	21	22	23	24	25	26	27	28	29	30	31	AUG
20	21	22	23	24	25	26	27	28	29	30	31	01	02	03	04	NOV
16	17	18	19	20	21	22	23	24	25	26	27	28	29	30		SEP
20	21	22	23	24	25	26	27	28	29	30	01	02	03	04		DEC
16	17	18	19	20	21	22	23	24	25	26	27	28	29	30	31	OCT
20	21	22	23	24	25	26	27	28	29	30	31	01	02	03	04	JAN
16	17	18	19	20	21	22	23	24	25	26	27	28	29	30		NOV
20	21	22	23	24	25	26	27	28	29	30	31	01	02	03		FEB
16	17	18	19	20	21	22	23	24	25	26	27	28	29	30	31	DEC
19	20	21	22	23	24	25	26	27	28	01	02	03	04	05	06	MAR

a

b

Persian Cats

C

d

e

f

g

h

i

k

p

q

r

S

t

u

$\mathcal{V}$

Persian Cats

Persian Cats

my cat's
health and
history

My cat's name ....

Date of birth ....

Birthplace ....

Sex ....

Colour of eyes ....

Colour of coat ....

Weight ....

Food favourites and hates ....

....

....

cat care
record

Dates of first vaccinations against :

Feline Influenza ....

Feline Infectious Enteritis ....

Annual booster due every ....

Worming tablets given ....

Birth of first litter...

Number of kittens ....

Date neutered ....

cat care
record

Name, address, and phone number of vet:

....

....

Dates of visits to the vet, and treatments prescribed:

....

....

....

....

Preferred cat sitters ....

....

....

Preferred catteries ....

....

....

....

Persian Cats